TOWARD AN ETHIC OF HIGHER EDUCATION

Toward an Ethic of Higher Education

Mortimer R. Kadish

Stanford University Press
Stanford, California
1991

Stanford University Press
Stanford, California
© 1991 by the Board of Trustees of the
Leland Stanford Junior University
Printed in the United States of America

CIP data appear at the end of the book

To Emilie

Acknowledgments

Two persons in particular own the indebtedness of this book. I gladly make them this unrequested and inadequate return of my acknowledgment. My colleague Raymond J. Nelson led me to the enterprise in the first place and sustained my interest afterwards. Through repeated discussion with him, I came to be aware of what I believe. My colleague and wife Emilie P. Kadish made innumerable careful and insightful suggestions for both the substance of this book and for its expression. Her hard criticism deserved a more adequate response than I could provide, her hard work a better outcome.

To my fellow students at the City College of New York before the outbreak of the Second World War I owe the first and final image of what a higher education might—just might—mean for its recipients. Their poverty, their anger at the injustice of the life around them, their determination to become what they would make themselves, their involvement in the wars of intellect and of party, their negations and their devotions, their often fierce debates, their irreverence and innocence, constitute the backdrop against which, and for the sake of which, the theses of this book were formed. If the remembrance is partly fancy, still what these people were, collectively, grounded the fancy.

To the successive generations of my own students I owe the constant, sometimes painful reminder that education is not a form of social reminiscence. They have made it clear to me that their changing demands, styles, manners, hopes, must be respected and provided for, that the very fact of change must be anticipated in the arrangements of higher education, lest the very demands, needs, aspirations, that each succeeding generation shares be frustrated.

My intellectual debt to John Dewey and George Herbert Mead is as deep as it will be obvious. Although much of what I have had to say would most certainly have been rejected with pointed emphasis (in different directions) by my teachers in philosophy, Morris R. Cohen, Ernest Nagel and Abraham Edel, not all would be by any means. The bits and pieces of the ethic I propose would not be conceivable without their influence and their example.

M.R.K.

Contents

Contents

TOWARD AN ETHIC OF HIGHER EDUCATION

Chapter One

Introductory: A Problem
and a Proposal

ON WHAT GROUNDS MIGHT American institutions of higher education decide among the major policy alternatives arising in the
conduct of that education, assuming those grounds are located
among the commitments of those institutions? How are we to
understand those alternatives and which among them shall we
choose? That is the twofold problem of this essay.

My end, therefore, is neither to canvas past or present opinion
on the nature of higher education nor to present a description
of higher education in America today, but to imagine the possible shape of an ethic of higher education. For such education,
I shall assume, implies, as do law or medicine, an ethic con-
straining the judgments of those who are or conceive themselves
responsible for its policies and their implementation. Like law
or medicine, higher education has assumptions of proper purposes, peculiar traditions, characteristic problems, possibilities
for extension or retrenchment, divisions, and dependencies and
interdependencies in relation to other social enterprises. This
being so, how might its practitioners conceive the choices of
their institutions in the conduct of education and what basic
standards and expectations would apply to their particular situation? These are determinations they must necessarily make if

they are to be practitioners rather than exploiters of their positions for private ends. They must formulate and reformulate the ethic of the practice they profess.

There is, of course, a question concerning the institutions to which the ethic would refer. Not every institution that calls itself a college, university, or institute commonly counts as one. Only those do that, focusing primarily on younger adults, demand of them a fairly high degree of intellectual activity in more or less recognized domains such as the so-called liberal arts and sciences, the professions, and the more complex technologies of the civilization. While such a criterion hardly draws a clear line in the sand, drawing one, fortunately, has little to do with formulating an ethic of higher education. To that end a few indisputable cases suffice to establish the species of institution where the practice of higher education could be said to occur. Private institutions like Columbia, Princeton, or Chicago, state institutions like the Universities of California and Michigan, colleges like Dartmouth or Oberlin, are, I take it, such cases. Other lists would serve equally well.

Vehement dispute exists even in these institutions about what goes into those "recognized" domains. I shall return to such disputes. They do not, however, diminish the utility of such institutions for fixing the reference of an ethic of higher education. That is because, first, one might expect general agreement that there is a class of studies that, deleted, would leave only the name of higher education; argument tends to be about the pertinence of further studies and the priorities granted them. Next, and perhaps more important, the very controversy about what our "civilization" is and ought to be, about what ought to be discarded and what cherished, marks, depending on how the argument is conducted, the existence of institutions such as those listed.[1]

Let there be, then, a further general restriction on the field of application of an ethic of higher education. Institutions of higher education are self-reflexive. They include, for our purposes, only those institutions that examine themselves and judge their own choice of policies.

The problem of the proper conduct of education is not, of course, that of higher education alone. As the disparity grows between what people must know to function effectively in a wealthy, competitive economy and what in fact they do know, between the skills required and the skills acquired, education generally has come under pressure. The rapid acceleration of high technology when organized schools are the primary means for transmitting and receiving the required skills forces the question of the responsible conduct of education increasingly upon our attention. The general public, along with its leaders, comes to worry more and more that America might cease to be Number One in the great football game of life. We hold schools responsible for our failures and possible successes alike. We argue that if only teaching methods, teachers, expenditures, and so on were improved, all losses would be restored and sorrows end. Only let the schools enable the citizenry to enter into the economy. Only teach them computing, mathematics, and the sciences. Fill their random access memories with megabytes of useful information. In that way, all—anyway, enough—will find Good Jobs and, on frequent paid vacations, join Melina Mercouri at a seashore magnificently improved even over the dream of the old movie.

One need not admire the hard sciences and high technology less to guess the practical consequences for the majority of making the business of education their service. Masters of little more than the skills necessary to balance a checkbook or do word processing, most can expect in the natural course of events only a long drift toward despair—with little to register in the checkbook, nothing to put on the monitor, and, for compensation, soaps, surrogate victories, and quiz show fortunes. Education conceived as the handmaid of technology now assures their self-rejecting, since it presents them to themselves as irrelevant to the expectations of a world they have been educated to accept. Given the normal curve and the steeply rising demands on most human capacities for effective participation in the system, both of which are fairly common knowledge, how could people think otherwise?

Two linked assumptions, I suggest, make it possible. People assume, first, that the accredited ends of society—a higher standard of living, greater equality among the citizenry, "democracy" in some sense, entrepreneurial prowess, efficiency, and so forth—jointly suffice to define the ends the community ought to serve. They also assume that all these ends can be secured simultaneously if only teachers do their job and enough are hired. They assume, in sum, that the business of education is to sustain the political, economic, and social status quo since otherwise the world as they know it falls apart. Unnoticed miseries for present people are easier to bear than doubt of this assumption.

To be sure, most purposes commonly held up for education—a decent income, for example—are hard to quarrel with. But that does not render all values of the social status quo either unambiguous, unassailable, or compatible with one another. Nor does it justify assuming that one and only one organization of society suits an information-revolutionized technology or even that every such revolution must ipso facto be desirable.

In this pass, might it not then seem plausible to replace a triumphant American status quo as the end of education with a nobler, more coherent, more persuasive dream? If the present is the trouble, try for another, better present. Let the appraisal of the choices of education wait upon the correct theory of the social good, and the acceptance of educational policies upon the general acceptance of that theory. First solve everything. The rest is easy. This approach, which indefinitely postpones addressing problems until they no longer exist, is familiar in the philosophy of education.

Devising a general social philosophy into which one's educational goals might fit is not, fortunately, the only alternative.

At least in higher education, I propose, another approach exists that locates the grounds for policy in the institutions of higher education. For in those institutions as they have developed within their cultures there is a tradition of relative autonomy from communal demands, a practice of academic freedom and of the defense of academic turf against the outside world that renders such an approach prima facie more plausible than it would be for primary and secondary schools. Rather than proceed from the ultimate ends and final context of human life to the alternatives of educational institutions, we reverse directions and begin, even if we do not end, with the commitments of those institutions as they stand. Having set aside the need to reinvent the moral universe, we find in higher education as it now exists issues for argument, constraints on discussion, and criteria by which to distinguish, however tentatively, some better positions from some worse ones. From these issues, constraints, and criteria will emerge, if we are fortunate, the changes and continuities that education might require.

The approach is not without precedent. Courts of law employ it when they reach judgments in the light of the argued entitlements as those entitlements have been interpreted and have evolved in the practice of the law. *Stare decisis*, the necessity to cohere with previous decisions, by restricting the relevance of possible issues and outcomes, makes the existence of determinate legal institutions possible. This hardly renders the general principles of morals, social philosophy, and economics logically irrelevant; the law in any stage of its development may lack the resources to ground a decision called for in an instant case without introducing new or revised principles. Even so, there is no need to invent the law from scratch, and particularly not when the legal system itself is conceived to embed certain general moral principles.[2]

Parallel considerations apply to higher education in the United States. One may seek, as in many a faculty argument, "the law" of that education in the precedents and principles embedded in its practices. When these do not decisively support one judgment or another, one reshapes principles, points out relationships among ends, reconstructs alternatives. The procedure is creative, yet not therefore groundless. Materials are there to be discovered and worked. That institutions of higher education, like legal institutions, embody challengeable customs, values, and objectives is the occasion and the point of development, not the end of the process. Certainly, in education as in law, the discovery that most judgments are challengeable, that there are often indeed pros and cons, will tempt some to replace the entire enterprise with a more complete and consistent alternative. Still, those tempted might well take note that most social revolutions salvage more of the system they rebel against than their proponents care to admit. There is no choice.

So much, then, for the first part of my proposal for an ethic of higher education, the institutional approach. The second part of my proposal is as follows. For the kinds of institution of higher education referred to, this essay selects as the principle for discriminating among policy choices the self-interest of those who do the job of education. Those who do that job are, of course, the students and faculty; administrators, trustees, legislatures, at best create the conditions for the performance of the job. The faculty's interest as faculty is that students learn what is in their self-interest to learn, and it is a part of the self-interest of students to know that they do not necessarily already know. Obviously, institutions of higher education have in fact many concerns other than education, concerns sometimes not entirely compatible with it. Here, however, I propose to assume that the self-interest of students rather than their manipulation for other purposes is central for determining the primary educational policies.

A long history of student demand and faculty response has embedded the priority of student interest in the educative processes of all serious institutions and sustains the assumption. Presidents, deans, and other academic statesmen regularly justify their policies by their utility to those in the classroom. Of course, if behavior is the sole criterion, they often do not believe their own pieties. Still, the bitterness of students and the cynicism of faculty testify to the depths of the perceived commitment of colleges and universities to take student interest seriously. I ask, therefore, what sorts of choices follow when one takes administrators at their word.

The commitment to student welfare, it should be understood, is in the role, not necessarily in the individual who occupies it. For students, faculty, and administration alike, it is comparable to the honor of soldiers who are not necessarily very brave or the rigor of scientists who bungle their inquiries. Without the role commitment of soldiers and scientists we have neither soldiers nor scientists. Without that of teachers and learners we have neither faculty nor students. Without a supporting role commitment of administrators we have the transmogrification of institutions of higher education into large, inefficient businesses.

A qualification is essential. Students have, as well as an interest in attaining their own welfare, an interest in seeking that welfare themselves. Those with a commitment to their welfare are therefore committed to the students' defining that welfare themselves. This is, after all, higher education. Adults or near-adults are its distinctive constituency. Adults are not simply beneficiaries to be acted upon for their own good; they make use of resources made available to them.

Some might doubt that the welfare of students actually is a serious commitment of actual institutions of higher education. Others might think that, even if it is, there are other commitments, like research, more important for the institution of higher education, or that it is a commitment better held in check. (Except in business, self-interest has a bad press.) Yet even these cannot afford not to know its implications for the educative process.

First, of course, anyone who cannot simply draft students and faculty had better understand what their interest might call for. The very survival of institutions of higher education depends upon some minimal consideration. But there is also a moral argument. When Kant laid down that it must be wrong to treat people merely as means, that one must treat them also as ends-in-themselves, he formulated a principle that could be accepted independently of considerations of technicalities of the pure reason. For surely any reasonably moral individual would want to put treating people as tools close to the essence of immoral activity. The question arises for anyone, then, what treating people as ends-in-themselves would entail in the context of higher education; and certainly that cannot exclude the consideration of their morally legitimate interests.

Even educators bemused by the role of higher education in facilitating new technologies and marketing strategies, competing with the Japanese, assuring American dominance in the world—or, for that matter, in providing suitable elites with cloisters for the pure play of disinterested minds and the contemplation of truth[3]—will, even if they are less than committed to a strict moral line, need to weigh the possible costs to human beings. Simple rationality, weighing costs against benefits, will require knowing the costs. Otherwise the decision makers cannot be sure of the hands-down primacy of the good they seek over the welfare of the individual selves they deal with. They must know what those rights and welfare amount to independently of the general good they are promoting. They cannot assume the simple reasonableness of asking people to work for the greater good of the economy, the glory of the nation, or the preservation of culture as though their own self-interest would follow automatically. Therefore, even proponents of those overriding interests require, to make their case, an inquiry into what sacrifices they are asking, for the sake of such interests, of those who engage in higher education.

Lastly, there is the possible ethical benefit of the inquiry into self-interest to be mentioned. Taking the self-interest of students and faculty seriously, if the interest of the self has to do with ethics, might be expected to throw some light on the relation of the enterprises of higher education to the ethical conduct of life. We ought not, as is frequently noted, to assume the crassness of self-interest unless the human self is crass. So Plato, arguing in the *Republic* that the self's interest implied justice and the other virtues, made the criterion of educational policies their ethical import. His error, from a modern point of view, lay not in his principle but in his advocacy of myth and indoctrination to achieve an ethical outcome, in his failure to see the essentiality of self-determination to self-interest in the educative process.

Nearly everyone, therefore, ought to find an enterprise such as this of fundamental interest. In following through on the choices in present-day higher education from the point of view of the self-interest of those involved, they would be following through on their concern with ethical judgment and ethical behavior. They might, conceivably, learn that ethics need not be relegated to primary and secondary schools if colleges and universities seek, like both Thrasymachus and Socrates, the self-interest of those involved. That Platonic possibility, as it seems only fair to call it, is more pertinent by far to discussions of higher education than the theory of Ideas. That it might be in some part realizable is a strong reason indeed for seeking an ethic of higher education in the light of the self-interest of its primary participants.

We may note that those running institutions of higher education who undertake to abide by such an ethic will spend some impossible hours seeking simultaneously to foster the welfare of the participants and to respect as an essential part of that welfare the freedom that participants are quite capable of turning against themselves. Their consolation will be that they, too, are fallible.

Two primary approaches to higher education in the United States constitute the immediate context in which this book is written. The self-interest of those who participate directly in higher education, and hence the ethic of higher education based upon that self-interest, owe a large part of their bearing upon contemporary discussion to their consequences for those approaches.

The first approach is, broadly, "intellectualistic." As used here, that is not quite the same as intellectual; higher education can have no quarrel with the interests of intellect or mind. An intellectualistic education turns the objects of those interests into objects of consumption to be grasped, contemplated, and appreciated. It aestheticizes. Colleges and universities become instruments for a restricted class of potential connoisseurs of certain rare and marvelous objects, and higher education's problem is to determine the objects best deserving appreciation.

Some half century ago Robert Hutchins broached a quasi-theological version of such an intellectualistic education. "Education implies teaching," he wrote. "Teaching implies knowledge. Knowledge is truth. The truth is everywhere the same. Hence education should be everywhere the same."[4] That those who teach know the "truth" is the interesting assumption. Presumably, truth would be found in the "classics," which of course are everywhere the same or they wouldn't be classics, and the truths of the classics would be the objects of aesthetic contemplation, appreciated and enjoyed for themselves.

In a well-known variation on the theme, Allan Bloom contends that higher education "is intended to encourage the non-instrumental use of reason for its own sake" and to "preserve the treasury of great deeds, great men and great thoughts."[5] "It must concentrate," he tells us, "on philosophy, theology, the literary classics, and on those scientists like Newton, Descartes and Leibnitz who have the most comprehensive scientific vision."[6] Of course, those named by Bloom created their classics in virtue of having used the past, aimed at the future, invented, reconstructed, and, in sum, systematically departed from the author's advice for the highly educated. Still, the heritage of "vision" and "great thoughts" remains the end on the consumer version of the business of higher education, and participants become the connoisseur curators of the treasury of human culture.[7] The university, we are told, "need not concern itself with providing its students with experiences that are available in a democratic society. They will have them in any event."[8]

The second approach with which these chapters take issue is probably more crucial for the contemporary scene where production tends to be of greater concern than refined consumption. Higher education cooperates by devoting itself to forming people who might be useful in a market economy. Scarcely a public utterance does not take what we may call the "practical approach" for granted. Practicality justifies the claims of math, physics, and the hard sciences—if not practical now, they will be eventually. Education has become, as is often enough proclaimed, investment, and to maximize production all must be afforded the opportunity to earn maximum bucks. Bits and pieces of an intellectualistic education are more or less acceptable on the periphery provided there is money for it, but the primary problem is to fix on what success in the economy would require. Since success these days may require assimilating much difficult material, practicality, looking far ahead and postponing gratification, justifies "higher" education in particular.

Enter now the multiversity, the university's heir. Practicality continues to be pursued and the ideal of equal opportunity treasured; but the practicality ministered to is expanded. At the multiversity, "higher" education ceases by definition to be tough the way math and physics are. Instead, programs are added. (On the fringes, junior colleges proliferate.) Refusing to work exclusively either for high-powered studies or for intellectualistic programs, education adds on indefinitely provision for desirable vocations.[9] The one becomes many. *Ex una plurimae.*

Jacques Barzun has some sharp and accurate exaggerations to offer on the subject: "the nearest equivalent to what the university is becoming is the medieval guild, which undertook to do everything for the town," he writes, quoting himself. "The only thing that the guild used to provide that we do not is Masses for the dead, and if we do not it is because we are not asked." [10] As I understand him, to restore some unity to the institution, resist the social and financial pressures, throw what weight remains to the university toward intellectual, though not intellectualistic, activities. Economize. Become one again, for the first time.

These pages do not propose shaving away at the multiversity with Barzun's razor. Some of what Barzun would take as mere accretions might well remain, given the financing. (When there is not enough financing, heaven help both the intellectual and the intellectualistic traditions—they, not the "accretions," will be the first to suffer unless they are technologically useful.) The unity envisaged here for the university and for higher education in general is of another order. For the "opening of the university" (described in Chapters 10 through 12), the point is not so much to eliminate the disunity and lack of focus a large variety of different enterprises may imply as to organize the disunity with a larger unifying view. In some measure, though only in some measure, opposition and disparity may become an opportunity for a further unity. We must see.

On the face of it, the grounds for the objection to both the intellectualistic and the practical or technological interpretations of higher education derive from the large and varied tradition of philosophical pragmatism in America—despite the scepticism that is also accepted here that intelligence and science suffice to resolve all or most of the problematic situations people face. No one should expect to find in these pages "the life of the mind" abstracted and impersonal, however fundamental intellectual activities are taken to be in a higher education. Rather it is the mind's "life" that is central—activity, change, creativity seen neither as wholly "instrumental" to other purposes nor as a pure act of self-expression for its own sake. What matters to the human understanding, and hence to higher education, matters to the human self in the formation of that self or it is not higher education.

Consider that marvel, all relevant knowledge made flesh. Some happy institution of higher education, recognizing great capacities, has made full use of them and now takes credit for his acquirements. Isaac Babel once wrote a story ("You Must Know Everything!") in which a grandmother insists that her grandson learn everything there is to know. That's him. All neural networks optimally stored, he sits by the TV watching the sitcoms like everyone else or thumbs through the mail-order catalogs before going back on the job. Nothing matters to him that did not already matter independently of his education. He stands on one side, his mind on the other. Isaac Babel's grand-mother would have drawn back at such a prospect. Who would want her prize educated to be a compact disk, even one loaded down with highly useful programs for doing this or that as well as with encyclopedic information? You buy disks. You give them to your kids.

Only the assumption that the population, except for its lack of information and techniques, is what it ought to be, a population chosen before all others for its wisdom and morality, makes the nightmare seem normal. Given such a population, education need only teach the majority how to get what it already wants. To be sure, anyone on remotely familiar terms with himself may never, by generalizing, reach to that assumption. Still, vanity and the marketing principle sustain it in the public mind. Politi-cal salespeople don't cross their customers. They stroke them.

One does not, in consequence of having rejected a certain kind of instrumentalism, therefore conclude with Allan Bloom that an institution of higher education ought to "encourage the non-instrumental use of reason for its own sake." To escape the nightmare of the purely instrumental mind, one does not need to presuppose uselessness. How an alternative to both sad con-clusions is possible, how it happens in the nonvocational heart

of the liberal, university education is one of our chief concerns
(Chapters 4 through 9).

First, however, I must reconsider (Chapters 2 and 3) the
nature of the self-interest in higher education upon which an
alternative ethic for the conduct of that education might rest.

Chapter Two

Positional Interests in Higher Education

THE SELF-INTERESTED POINT of view in the context of higher education would demand the satisfaction of what I shall call "the positional interests" of the participants in the educative process. These interests are what would be to the individual's advantage in relation to the opportunities and restrictions of the institutions of higher education.

The interest in salvation, if there were such a thing as salvation, would be nonpositional. Everybody would have it. The interest in eating or having sex or surviving is nonpositional also. You don't have those interests in virtue of any social position you enjoy or suffer. Similarly for the interest, if there is any such specific interest, in being happy. (That people want desperately to be happy without knowing what that happiness would consist in suggests that the desire is, rather than an interest, at best a motivation of some sort and at worst a form of despair.) The only relevance of nonpositional interests here is their possible bearing upon the positional interests we adopt.

Positional interests are had as a such and such: doctor, lawyer, beggarman, thief. They are yours insofar as, for whatever reason, you identify yourself with the role: "I am a doctor, a lawyer, a beggarman, a thief; that's what I am, or maybe a number of them." As a such and such you want certain things to happen. You assume the position.

Sometimes, of course, as when drafted into the army, you don't assume the position at all; it is assumed for you. Then, while you are in the position of someone who has the positional interests of a soldier, those positional interests are yours only in an external sense. You do what as a soldier you have to do and also what you can to get out.

But if you do assume the position, you have a positional interest in the achievement of the ends of your position or role in a social institution engaged in a certain sort of practice. To judge from that position is to judge from self-interest, even when the judgments are counterproductive. You are out for yourself as a such and such. If it runs counter to your welfare as an individual to occupy that position, then you ought to assume one more congenial.

Higher education is a practice like any other. Students and faculty define themselves by the interests they have in virtue of their positions as students and faculty. Their "self-interest" affords working criteria for the judgment of educational policy not only for them but for all those whose judgments bear upon the policies of higher education: faculty outside their instructorial roles; administration; trustees; the public that supports that education. The reason is that a positional interest exists in virtue of its acceptance within the institution as an interest of that institution and on that basis extends its claim to consideration. Those who deny its legitimacy but claim to support the institution are less than truthful.

At the same time that the requirements of positional interests impose criteria upon the major policy choices, they impose only a claim to serious consideration. Positional interests are not preemptive. While all—faculty, administration, students— have, insofar as they are concerned, an obligation to respect the realization of that interest, other interests, such as the faculty's in working in the arts and sciences, are also legitimate in the institution. Institutional governance, therefore, must allocate to the various legitimate claims their due weight. The positional interests of students and their instructors do not suffice to say how universities might best weigh their requirements against the requirements of other interests. Still, they must be heard. What do they say?

These, on the present account, are the interests of the participants in institutions of higher education insofar as those institutions concern themselves with higher education: (1) an interest in students preparing themselves for effective participation in the society they are about to enter; (2) an interest in students reaching a decision about what they actually want both for themselves in society and for themselves as civilized human beings if, as is likely, they do not already know; (3) a derivative interest in the coherence of the first two interests. The first I call the interest in "effectiveness," the second in "self-formation," or, more briefly, in self, the third, of course, in coherence.[1]

I have spoken, advisedly, of the positional interests of participants, rather than simply of students. For I want to say more than that faculty's function is to help achieve the self-interest of the students as exhibited in their positional interests. Taxi drivers are concerned to get us to our destination, but to say that their self-interest is to secure ours is an obvious exaggeration. Faculty members, however, are not like taxi drivers. It is important to their self-interest as faculty that, in securing the positional self-interest of the students, they are securing the welfare of those students. To emphasize that is the reason for speaking of the interests of the participants rather than simply of the students.

To understand the sense in which these same interests characterize both students and their instructors, we begin by noting that every interest has an objective and a beneficiary. The objective is the state of affairs that satisfies the interest, the beneficiary the individual or group advantaged by that objective.

If, for example, I am a member of the Democratic party, my objective as a member of that party is the achievement of its goals. I may or may not be a beneficiary of those goals. Even if a less regressive tax benefits me, the objective of the Democratic party's interest that as a member I share is not my benefit, but a less regressive tax structure. Though I might have joined the party for the sake of that or some other benefit, that benefit is not my objective as a member but my motivation for joining. The relation between benefit and the attainment of the objective of that membership is contingent. I am, as it were, the contingent beneficiary.

Consider, on the other hand, hospital patients. They have a positional interest in *their* being made well and a consequent claim on the hospital to do what it can for them. They are the necessary beneficiaries of their positional interest, the object of their own interest; benefit and interest are one, and motivation is beside the point. Even if they came into the hospital for all sorts of crazy reasons, insofar as they are patients, *their* health is still their positional interest. There can be no question of a distinction between the welfare of the patients and the objective of the medical practice.

Students are more like patients at a hospital than like members of the Democratic party. They too are necessary beneficiaries of their positional interest. One expects them to look out for themselves in the relevant ways. Student positions and patient positions differ, however, not only in the substance of their objectives but also in that the autonomy of patients, like that of children in a family, may tend to cut very little ice. The autonomy of students, on the other hand, is a vital part of their positional interests. Colleges, having recognized that students are the necessary beneficiaries of their own interest, often conclude that it is their duty to act in loco parentis, which implies acting regardless of the wishes of the students. But students who in their role themselves aim at their own welfare cannot, in the effort to secure it, surrender their autonomy to the instructor.

The instructors cannot be like physicians in their entrepreneurial role selling services of which the patient is the necessary beneficiary. (That these services produce health is no doubt indispensable to their sale, but profit, not health, is the objective of entrepreneurs.) They must be more like the hospital staff or physicians in their position as healers, with the important difference that they recognize student autonomy. If the students' well-being in the relevant ways were not their objective, instructors would be no more than employees or a loosely organized group of merchants. Their position would be destroyed, and their institution's commitment to student interest would be rendered meaningless.

That the faculty role in the educative process is more than instrumental will make sense once it is understood that one may simultaneously have a duty to promote a welfare, as faculty do, and a welfare interest in the achievement of that welfare. So students can, and often do, demand—not merely hope—that faculty share with them, if in lesser degree, their own interest in themselves. Institutional hiring policies might properly be skewed to increase the chances of taking on in the educator's role only those persons who conceive their own welfare as at least partly satisfied by the satisfaction of their interest's primary beneficiaries.

The point is not that faculty members are or ought to be upscale versions of Mr. Chips. If they regard the achievement of the welfare of their students as part of their own, and hence directly in their self-interest, other central academic interests —the advancement of their disciplines, preeminently—may still dominate their lives. Even so, one must not overlook the simple preference for the welfare over the ill fare of others that David Hume made central to the possibility of morality even when interests diverged and clashed.[2] That we may benefit, not only each one separately as the final consequence of working together, but also each directly and immediately by virtue of the benefit afforded the other, makes a shared human life possible.

A relation of human persons, not merely of rational agents, is forged. So faculty may regard students as persons and, it is to be hoped, students regard faculty in the same way. Each group finds in the welfare of the other at least a modest part of its own. (None of this, of course, is to deny the place of instrumental relations in education as elsewhere. Purely instrumental relations, candidly accepted as such, as in the relation of buying and selling, often turn out to everyone's good. Higher education need not celebrate a common humanity at every point any more than any other human relationship does.)

Faculty and student, however, share the same positional interests, and not only in the sense that faculty finds in the welfare of students some portion of its own good. Faculty may also become the direct beneficiaries of the educative process. To be sure, if they are any good at all, instructors are unlikely, except in certain phases of graduate study, to be particularly advantaged by the information and skill that may come their way from the student side. Still, they may actually be direct beneficiaries of the educative process in another way. They too are persons. They are not immune to interest in themselves because they are faculty. They may work for themselves in the interchange, learn and unlearn their own wants, and hope that their coparticipants may also at times see them as learners and inquirers who put themselves on the line. They may become, so to speak, their own secondary beneficiaries. The point will recur.

Now let us reconsider the particular interests of the participants in the educative process.

Given their interest in "effectiveness," students may legitimately require that the educative process be evaluated by whether it offers the means for getting the skills, information, and attitudes necessary for a successful life of the sort they want. They have an inevitable interest in the effectiveness of the educative process for careers in the professions or business, or even, though no longer frequently, for a career as a lady or a gentleman.

To become effective, students also need credentials. Credentials often enough have only the most general relationship to the practices to which they permit access. Nevertheless, society demands them as a guarantee of relevant skills, attitudes, and information. Even if the guarantee fails, however, the need for credentials shows very clearly the nature of the interest in effectiveness. For in the seeking of credentials, the focus falls not on the self's being prepared to take its part in society but on the demands of society, whatever one may think of them.

This external focus of any interest in effectiveness holds no matter how difficult people find the skill or information required. When one learns to finger a violin, one's fingers and one's clumsiness become objective facts. One swears at them and sweats. They have become the problem out there, to be dealt with. In failing or succeeding, the self measures itself against socially given criteria. Seeking effectiveness, it places itself, not the criteria, on trial.

And now the trial itself, having forced the individual's self-reassessment, leads away from the objective conditions for effectiveness to a reconsideration of what that individual might want. The attempt at effectiveness has led to the next major concern to which a higher education devotes itself: away from the concentration on the world as the source of standards to the interest in self-formation and what the self really wants.

One may not know the course by which to reach a particular end state. One may wonder whether to try for medical or law school as a result of uncertainty about the chances of admission and the likelihood of one or the other bringing in the larger income. But that is not the only way students show that they don't know what they want. They may not know what end state to want. Not their calculations but their "values," as we say, remain undetermined. They don't know *what* they want. (Neither, of course, do many older people.)

Self-interest, therefore, engenders an inevitable interest in constructing those norms that will support—or undermine—acting for income or some other end. Just who, one needs to know, might one be? People may, and do, become problems for themselves in a way no amount of introspection or self-palping will resolve. Their only recourse in their perplexity will be to seek self-formation and re-formation through interaction with their worlds. In pursuing their interest in themselves, they may learn what they want; learning what it is, they will know who they are.

I emphasize again that in higher education the participants' interest demands that *they* choose and, in their capacity as free agents, enter into inevitable conflict. Students must resist their teachers, their teachers must resist them. Concessions must be granted, not coerced. Compliance as such to the will of one side or the other, though it may often enough happen, ends the educative game. Their self-formation left to others, participants approximate the condition of many hospital patients; lacking an effective voice, they find their positional interest diminishing into a positional hope.

But the college or university is no hospital. Indeed, the interest in self requires more even than that participants in the educative process refuse to become patients. They may not even deal with themselves as their own patients, as subject matter for themselves. They may not, if the processes of education are to be effective, become their own fictions to be written as the imagined requirements of their art dictates. They must seek themselves rooted and defined in their objective circumstances.

Let us remind ourselves of the kind of circumstances that make the forming and re-forming of the self and its wants possible in higher education. Not only may effectiveness blocked compel individuals to revise wants and reorder priorities. That legitimate interest in effectiveness, even when satisfied, may not suffice to determine all a self's wants and priorities. For some, to be sure, a central end or career may indeed organize all significant wants. A "born" dancer may live to dance; a Mozart will do what he must. Interest in self has here been satisfied. But for those without a clear and powerful central end organizing all significant wants there are only restlessness, pervasive dissatis-faction, ill-formed wants, and the sense of a basic inadequacy. This confusion and malaise notwithstanding, such individuals can assume some initial basis, however ill formed and inade-quate, for approaching the new occasions of their lives. They have preferences along with their instinctual drives; and these, under the influence of education, they work and rework.

More particularly, participants in the educative process mea-sure themselves against an initial image of themselves. They think they are doing better when they satisfy that image; they are pleased with themselves when they do, disappointed in them-selves when they do not. They are quite capable, therefore, of distinguishing between the brute fact of wanting something and a want of which they approve, and all too aware that some-times their wants will not do. Then, to make them do, they will modify the very way they see themselves. Among the factors that drive the self to re-form itself, self-disdain is as central as the desire for self-approval.

The most obvious among the circumstances that make the forming and re-forming of the self possible in higher education must be the explosion of possibilities. In the course of their edu-cation, students encounter options they had previously never thought of or understood—not just career options but ways of judging those options and, in general, splendid and frighten-ing expectations of life and of themselves. Such unimagined or transformed possibilities re-make judgments and lives. Alter-natives have proliferated, refined. New consequences alter de-sires. Persons become other than they were in their very modes of identifying themselves to themselves. There is no need to "teach" values for values to be acquired. The old self expands, explodes, with the old world. For this reason one can conceive of the educative process not just as adding, subtracting, or modi-fying wants but as re-forming the self itself.

None of this presumes that self-formation in higher education has much effect on the levels of the self that concern the psychologist and psychoanalyst. It is not supposed to have any such effect. But that higher education is not a form of therapy in no way diminishes its relevance to the way in which real individuals might use and misuse their endowments and their weaknesses, their sickness and their health, in a newer, braver world.

We are brought to the third positional interest of participants in the educative process: the coherence of the interests in effectiveness and self each with the other and each, since each is complex, within itself. For not all wants can be simultaneously satisfied, and even those that do not conflict are apt to suffer frustration. In consequence, the institution of higher education that forms its policies on the basis of the participants' interest confronts systematically the pervasive and unending problem of the factual disjointedness of human ends (conceived as the satisfaction of our wants) and means; and it must seek to anticipate the future.[3]

There are three basic kinds of incoherence. The first kind is familiar enough. Institutions of higher education are to a greater or lesser degree perpetually attempting to key their preparations to what the profession or other future activity envisaged by students requires. In consequence, given their fallibility, they may land the individual entering on his new life either badly prepared or in a life situation for which he or she is basically unfit, or both. The person's freedom has been respected, the person's welfare defeated. Such are the inevitable facts of life.

The second kind of incoherence is less familiar. Everybody expects that higher education will shape what people become. But that it may also shape wants never to be satisfied or wants that conflict—that, in brief, higher education assiduously pursued might mess people up—educators less often advertise. They like to pretend that at the college or university one might expect to win the highest stakes of civilization, provided one does the right things, without chancing a heavy cost. But the good might become, like Moses, strangers in a strange land. Not only may these cultivated ones under the influence of their education cease to know what they would want for themselves in the world they find; in the world they find they may undergo conflicts of loyalties, crises of conscience. Having recognized the plural allegiances defining their identities, they may find the fidelity to themselves that is self-interest in action beyond their grasp.

The third kind of incoherence consists in that factual disjointedness of ends and means that higher education unavoidably faces in a quarrel between the requirements of effectiveness and the interest in self. Having established the conditions for the achievement of effectiveness, it may have weakened those required for the identification of the self within the civilization. Having achieved those conditions making for that identification, it may have weakened the conditions for effectiveness. Having struggled to meet both of its commitments to the participants in the educative process, higher education may achieve neither. The warfare of complex perspectives and brute practices is an old story. Circumstance *will* have it so.

More will be said later of ways in which institutions might respond, not indeed to eliminate all chance of incoherence— to attempt that one would need to convert huge societies like the Soviet Union, which has tried something of the sort, into so many wildly expanded Platonic republics—but to minimize the chances of the worst disasters. Meanwhile, it is important to note that all three of the related forms of incoherence may become sources of creativity as well as of disaster. Incoherence in individual and social life might, under propitious circumstances, issue in a radical transformation of person and society as well as of the immediate situation; one ought not, if one could— and one cannot—eliminate from individual or social life every chance of incoherence. Furthermore, one might reasonably seek instead the application of knowledge and policies that would at once minimize the probabilities of the worst disasters for individuals and institutions while fostering the strength and imagination needed for creative action. Such difficult demands, of course, define a direction only. That the best to be hoped for is only a rough and temporary approximation does not diminish the importance of the direction.

In broad terms, then, the positional interests of the participants in higher education and the many policy decisions that may or may not lead to such ends are, finally, the grounds for criticizing the technologization of education and its confinement to a cloistered liberal arts alike. It remains to say why one might be inclined to accept them, all three, rather than some other conception of what self-interest might mean in higher education. For the fact that an interest is embedded in practice is never in itself sufficient to justify that interest, however many the tied in considerations that must be accounted for before the interest is modified or superseded.

Let us recall, first, that the positional interests of students and faculty in the educative process are, in a fundamental respect, unlike those of members of the American Medical Association, the Teamster's Union, or the Farm Bureau. People call the latter "special interests," having in mind that they compete more or less directly with other interests. They are properly wary of taking such interests as data in the analysis and evaluation of the economic process because these interests may contravene both other special interests and the common interests of the community. The positional interests of student and faculty as such, however, aiming as they do directly at the essential human welfare of students and faculty, stand in basic accord with the interests the community holds in common in a civilized society. Nor do they pose any immediate threat to the various special interests, unless those special interests oppose community interests. Benevolence and the general good, in brief, favor the student and faculty interests, assuming a willingness to put up with the expense of higher education.

Next, members of a free society must find it attractive that neither the interest in effectiveness nor the interest in self exacts systematic faith or submission as the price of the participants' welfare. The first specifically places students in a position to secure their own welfare through the choice of an appropriate preparation. The second recommends itself even more strongly on that same principle of self-determination. Nobody functions as a self-interested self if, in self-formation and the deciding of what ends to choose, one does not have the final judgment. It must strongly recommend these first two positional interests that the very conduct of our lives as adults calls for them, and strongly recommend the third that it aims at making the achievement of ends possible.

The recommended positional interests have the further advantage of making a certain amount of sense both of the history of higher education and of its current programs. So the medieval university can be understood to aim preeminently at effectiveness. The profoundly ahistorical concept of society and humanity that prevailed would have made an interest in self-formation unintelligible. The question of the legitimacy or desirability of a choice of values was, in theory, solved. The Church had solved it; the rest was discipline.

In nineteenth-century England and subsequently, a different dream of education took shape. The university, aiming at preparing gentlemen and eventually ladies, prepared them first in Latin and Greek and then expanded the curriculum without therefore necessarily changing the objective. The overriding objective was the forming of selves and the fixing of types of wants. People as unlike as Cardinal Newman and John Stuart Mill agreed that engineering and the other "mechanical" arts had no place in a proper higher education.[4] The divergence between effectiveness and the interest in self became a matter of principle, reenforcing the class structure that made it possible.

Higher education in America today attempts to preserve, and transform, both traditions. Now such phenomena as the acceleration in the possibilities and demands of technology, the growth of democracy, and the increasing power of the mass market suborn and transform values and make a resolution of the tension between effectiveness and the interest in self through separate programs devoted to one or the other less and less the obvious course. An M.I.T.—and not only an M.I.T.—will extend its concern into the humanities. At the same time, no liberal arts institution will entirely neglect the question of career preparation. Programs at most institutions become at once complex and up for grabs. Unexpected subject matters obtrude; the humanities give. In brief, the task of reconciling effectiveness and the interest in self now constitutes the distinctive problem of the modern institution of higher education.

There is, of course, no a priori reason to pay any attention to the problem simply because it is distinctive. One might, to put the matter in extreme form, choose business school and resolve the question of what to want by assuming it as settled that money is the answer. Or one might aim at the sensitized consciousness of a liberal education and let the recipient sink or swim. Pay your money and take your choice. Still, it is an advantage to our account of the positional interests of students and faculty that it provides an expanded map of the choices of higher education for our exploration.

Chapter Three

Questioning Growth

THE QUESTION IS WHETHER one can derive a map for the choices of higher education from the concept of growth. Growth, according to the pragmatic tradition in America, is the goal of all education. Sidney Hook, writing in that tradition, defines growth as "the maturation of man's natural powers toward the highest desirable point which his body, his mind, and his culture make possible."[1] "Higher" education, on this view, would seek this maturation on a more intellectually demanding level and in this way serve both the self-interest of students and the interests of a democratic society. As John Dewey puts it, "The criterion of the value of school education is the extent to which it creates a desire for continuous growth and supplies means for making the desire effective in fact."[2] The participants in the educative process have a positional interest in growth.

Now, my thesis is that the participants have an interest in growth but not a positional one. To say that in no way denigrates the value of the concrete changes in people to which growth in the pragmatic tradition refers; it merely denies the serviceability of the idea in the projecting of educational policies in certain kinds of institutions. Not only are the interests in effectiveness, self-formation, and coherence not just aspects of growth, the differences are essential in determining what, from the point of view of the participants, would constitute the proper choice of major policies in higher education.[3]

In support of this general view I begin by considering some prima facie difficulties with the general notion of growth as the object of the participant's interest in higher education and then suggest a conception of a human self which explains why one ought to expect those difficulties. From that conception will follow an alternative to growth as the proper expectation of participation in the educative process.

Prima facie, self-interested persons unclear to begin with about what they want will have no way of saying what their "growth" might be or what might foster or curtail it; the reference to growth has become inoperative just where their problem in self has become critical. Where their wants are clear and given, of course, the case is different; they can track their progress, they have their standards. But where those ordering wants that form their standards are in question, people cannot know whether they have succeeded in "growing," only that they have succeeded in changing. If, for whatever reason, they find themselves approving of their changed selves, perhaps they will call the change growth.

It seems otherwise, perhaps, because of assumptions about the criteria for growth in human beings. Human beings are said to "grow" when, for example, they become more sensitive, more aware. But a variety of circumstances over which they have no control might lead to very different judgments about the changes in sensitivity and awareness that they have undergone. When is sensitivity neurotic and awareness a disaster? It is commonly understood that the more sensitive and informed people become in the course of education, the more vulnerable they become as well, and the more demanding of their environments. Often, greater sensitivity and awareness are eminently worth the price. But, depending on circumstances, this may not be the case. Increased vulnerability is not as such growth. When to so judge it is a pivotal question.

Growth on the classic view (which, with its biological orientation, differs from the Deweyan view) implies a flowering or realization of human nature. For human beings, however, one flowering or realization has as a frequent condition the destruction of another. Selves are complex. Their wants are not necessarily mutually sustaining, as are the biological wants that sustain the organism. Actual circumstances rarely permit a balanced ecology of desire. In the application of the notion of growth, therefore, serious disagreements may be expected over which "natural" interests are prior "naturally." What would justify one preference over another? The participants in a higher education usually do not even know the cost; and, except in the broadest terms, they often do not know the self-realizations they prefer until after they have realized themselves. A properly organized higher education will not seek to select in advance the flowerings of its participants. It will leave that to them.

The problem is not only that circumstances are frustrating and cruel. Their very kindness may foreclose growth and do so by leaving too much open. For to become anything in particular positively entails the active cultivation of an increasing *incapacity* for flowerings and realizations that were perhaps once achievable. In the very processes of higher education, and all through life, not only do possibilities close down; we are lost unless they do. One narrows one's field of vision, willingly. One "majors"! When Dewey affirms that "we have laid it down that the educative process is a continuous process of growth, having as its aim at every stage an added capacity for growth,"[4] self-interest itself objects. It objects not simply to the supposed continuity of the process; it objects in the general interest of being a determinate self. The end "at every stage" cannot be "an added capacity for growth," not where self-construction is the end. Sometimes, no matter the costs, we can grow no further. We *have* grown, and to attain that state is at some stages the hoped-for end of a genuinely self-interested person.

The chief prima facie difficulty, however, may be a practical one. Seeking to apply the notion of growth, educators in higher education seem to have no recourse but to locate growth in a more or less continuous movement toward satisfying established expectations. The student, for example, grows as grades improve; if grades are distrusted, the student grows as it would have been determined that he or she had if grading systems were adequate. The individual's growth as an individual becomes in practice the sum of movements toward the satisfaction of the sets of established expectations. Then, to defend the expectations, one talks of the growth of the person; but the lines of development are given. Growth as a process means molding the self according to a given pattern at that point, crucial for higher education, when biology does not suffice to distinguish between the natural and unnatural. "Growing," the individual pitches in, works with the decisions that have already been made. What development "ought" to be, if it is not to be unnatural, is preordained.

The denouement soon follows. Seeking to grow in conformity with their nature, people seek to discover the requirements of that nature in the identification with one or another established type. This they do at just the points when who and what they are become most problematic; they ask for what are called "role models." Role models are followed, even if first they are chosen; in that choice people settle the practical problem of growth. Because they desperately hope to grow, they demand role models to fix what they shall be. Tell them what to be. Better still, show them. Show them the word made flesh. Or give them alternative models, a menu appropriate for persons such as they. Role models are for the compliant when the expected futures have ceased to be acceptable. Higher education would seem to have as its business not the provision of role models but their criticism and a passage beyond them.

Growth, then, as a criterion at least of higher education in the sense intended here seems not to do. Higher education, taking over just at the point where natural processes and conventional agreement cease to fix the definition of growth, cannot find in growth an adequate objective for the welfare of persons in the educative process.

Another fundamental circumstance, the consequences of which must now be considered, underlies the above judgment and leads to an alternative criterion for educational policies. The fact that human selves are functions of human individuals in changing and disruptive social contexts, not biological or spiritual givens that find one milieu more favorable than another, more or less frustrating, more or less "growth" inducing, gives rise to what I call the thesis of sociality. This thesis offers no particular ontology either of minds or selves. Rather, it designates the phenomena connected with human sociality that make minds or selves the problems they are. (That human beings are intrinsically social is in itself, of course, utterly familiar to Dewey and his many followers. Any break with him and others in the tradition emerges over the consequences for self-interest of a human sociality formulated from a less cheerful perspective than his.) The following constitute the salient positions of this thesis:

1. "Self" designates whatever people refer to when they say such things as, "This is *my* interest, *I* want this or that." "Self-interest" is the interest of selves. People don't mean by it "This is my body's interest," or they would never regard it as to their interest to do anything contrary to the health of their bodies. Instead, the functioning of the body constitutes one of *their* interests. The body in question, as they say, *belongs* to me; I *myself* have a body, whatever "I" am. Similarly, they speak of "you" and "yours," "them" and "theirs," "her" and "hers," and so on. First person, second person, and third person imply one another.

Sometimes, particularly when referring to higher education, people refer to "minds" rather than selves. The effect is then to separate out what are conceived as purely intellectual aspects of the self from the self's feelings, aesthetic perceptions, loves, revulsions, individual identity. When "mind" alone becomes the province of higher education, "self-interest" becomes the antithesis of what higher education is about. The observations in this book entail the systematic rejection of that antithesis.

2. Even though selves do not grow like human bodies or potted plants, according to developmental, biological laws, biological and psychological mechanisms do impose significant constraints on their development. That changes in social environment can fashion human beings regardless of built-in genetic constraints on the wants of individuals or populations is a patent myth. On the other hand, since biology and, to a lesser extent, psychology seem to be far more directly tied to the development of children than adults (adults being presumed to have more or less completed their development), satisfying built-in constraints on what people want or need to grow would seem more pertinent to the education of children than to that of adults and near-adults.

For persons of any age, however, the very possibility of the achievement of self is built into the organization of the brain. The human nervous system incorporates the resources needed for the construction of different lives or, if one prefers, the realization of different programs. The laws of biological development themselves provide the differing neural networks that respond to different conditions and generate different selves.[5]

3. Those networks generate these selves in a complex interaction within a changing social milieu that, for the purposes of education, is found to subsist in the *import* of the behavior of individuals for one another. In consequence of that import, human relationships generate selves, and the relations among selves become, precisely, "interpersonal"—relations among *persons*. Actions have their interpersonal import in virtue of a common language of gestures, linguistic and otherwise, established in the community and its institutions.[6] As a result, self-formation occurs both in formal education and outside it, not

through the addition of information bytes to a preprogrammed self but through the meaning ascribed to the information in a relevant grammar. The concept of education as the transmission of information therefore misses the point. Education so conceived deals with persons as though they were machines manipulating uninterpreted symbols, not conferrers of meaning. *Babette's Feast*, an unusual recent movie, illustrates the point. Babette's guests do not simply satisfy their hunger, although of course they do that. The food is delicious. They become aware that they are at a feast. They become, by degrees, increasingly aware of one another, open to one another when before they were opaque. They are persons, the food is heaven, they come together finally in a kind of agape. At the end, the heavens themselves in their eyes thicken with stars; the lame skip and jump. The food they savored *meant* . . . they hardly knew what. It "meant" in virtue of a community of dreams and religious resonance.

The phenomenon is completely general. Human beings who rape or murder perform an act rather than a reflex satisfying a certain description. They perform a gesture; and, as human beings, comprehend themselves in terms of that gesture and its relation to others.

Higher education expands and complicates, beyond the routines of everyday life, the context in which behaviors are comprehended as gesture, hence realized as human behaviors.

4. Because that context, or grammar, is under historical conditions "self-contradictory"—neither all of a piece nor always coherent, and almost never static—what people make of themselves and what they want tend to have similar characteristics.[7] They find themselves not knowing what they want, what they are doing, or how to define themselves to themselves. Self-formation becomes an irresistible problem. Were history false and life in society a ceaseless round of fixed alternatives in established circumstances, people might sometimes condemn

themselves for forbidden drives or impulses. But they would not question what they were to want or in what terms to understand those wants.

It is here, in the assessment of the prospects for individuals of inadequacy and internal conflict, that this book departs from the American tradition of social pragmatism. Where a John Dewey finds the condition and promise of progress in the remaking of "indeterminate" and "problematic" situations, the thesis of sociality as a thesis for selves removes the necessary basis for a progressive resolution for every remaking of the self and its situation. Hence it disputes not just the practical likelihood of progress but also its criteria, and it disputes the case for growth as the encapsulation of those criteria.[8]

On this account of the self and the conditions of its development, the three positional interests are distinguishable from any interest in growth as the principal determinant of the policies of higher education. Growth is not, as it might be argued, just another way of saying self-formation. Nor is distinguishing between the two to make too fine a point of it. Growth as the objective for higher education may actually conflict with an interest in self-formation that demands the formation of the self *by the self.* For growth, unless under extremely favorable conditions of social life, might demand fundamental control over both the social environment and those with whom the educational contract is made; and that would radically alter the nature of the institutions of higher education and of the society. In general, the power, wisdom, and control needed to secure growth in the face of human and social incoherence are overwhelming. Institutions committed to the positional interest in self-formation will, on surrendering any dream of becoming successors to Plato's Republic or of functioning within a Deweyan democracy, find themselves as a matter of principle surrendering, from time to time, decisions they may have derived from some theory of growth.

Self-determination aside, however, higher education could still not reasonably expect to make good upon any implicit contract with those participating in the educative process to secure their welfare for them. No set of policies, regardless of their rigor, could suppress wildly varying initial conditions all through the course of human careers. Human involvement in language and society would continue to generate self-systems too sensitive to the slightest fluctuations in their environments, defeating the most rational of managements.

Now add that higher education *on principle* makes every effort to expose its participants to possibilities in life and culture on a level and in a dimension that they had not, before their involvement, really begun to conceive. Institutions call the exposures opportunities. Yet the more complex a system, the more unstable. The more institutions promise, the more they insure their inability to keep their promises. Prediction, hence control, becomes possible only in the most general terms; the sensitivity and unpredictability that distinguish the young person's career have made the growth of the self under most of the circumstances of higher education as intrinsically questionable as long-range forecasts of the weather.[9]

The relationship of growth and the positional interest in coherence is now apparent. Growth makes coherence a precondition of the process of education rather than an essential determinant of the process itself, a situation which, from the point of view of the thesis of sociality, will not do. From that point of view, given what it means to be a self in a changing social matrix, coherence can never be presupposed. Instead, it is something achieved or lost in a process of education, an interest guiding, shaping the education as it is brought into play. Those who fix on growth as the business of education do not take incoherence seriously enough as a problem in education. It is central.

Neither do they take seriously enough the implications of effectiveness. Becoming effective through a vocation or profession is commonly thought part of a maturation process—"normal" growth. There is no objection to talking this way given certain assumptions about the vocation or profession. Clearly, ineffectiveness is a fundamental harm to anybody and deadly to growth under most definitions. But that it is therefore to be avoided at any cost is unclear.

Everything depends on the conditions for effectiveness encountered in the world. The traditional warning against selling one's soul or, in modern jargon, selling out, makes the point. One can sell out in perfectly respectable ways, depending on who and what one has become, but that does not make it less selling out. Hence, while becoming effective is a legitimate enough interest, it cannot be automatically subsumed under growth except in the conventional sense in which becoming an adult is part of growth, and no one can be an adult without being in some way and in some degree effective.

These problems with growth and the disparity between growth and the positional interests provide a basis for discriminating an alternative image of higher education. What, we may now ask, might sociality and the positional interests actually imply for the legitimate expectations of the participants?

An institution of higher education is less like a brave new world than a gambling house in which self-interest itself, not cash, is wagered on the games. The main difference, aside from the games played, is that, unlike most gambling houses, the house of education tries, so far as the integrity of the game permits, to work the odds in the gambler's favor. There is no doubt that this makes for a most unusual gambling house. But then I have never denied that higher education works for the benefit of the participants; I have merely refused to identify that benefit with the nonpositional interest of growth.

The positional interests assure gambles, not victories. The very process of furthering the self-interest of the participants in the educative process offers them only uncertain outcomes.

Colleges and universities wager that their spread of gambles will serve those persons qualified to participate more than would just one large bet, taken on registration, that the house will succeed in achieving their welfare. They deny that among the many games the house offers they must ensure that the players choose the games with the happiest outcomes for them. They acknowledge that this is beyond them.

The name of the higher education for which growth is the criterion is Alma Mater. Many colleges and universities conceive of themselves, or pretend to, in her image: the bountiful, nourishing Mother, she who has your good at heart, who spreads the table. Eat, eat my children! She has had the diet designed by the wisest men and women. Grow a good, strong head on your shoulders. Cooperate. Measure up. For your own sake. As your parents cared for you when you were younger, now she does. Translation: Growth is your positional interest. Those who run this institution to the best of their ability do not offer gambles for making or (and this is essential) unmaking yourself. Alma Mater, being who she is, offers only opportunities for making yourself, even if some of these opportunities, given human fallibility, are flawed.

Of course, Alma Mater has more than one face; the self-making opportunities, depending on the institution, may be for any number of things besides "growth." They may be for salvation. They may be for membership in a class or a people. They may be for a military career. Our business, our self-interest at the institution, is to seize the opportunity of our happy position.

There are two possible conceptions, then, of educational institutions. One offers many bets in many games; the other, one overriding bet that you can make it. If in educational institutions we choose the former, we bet on the provision of opportunities for self-formation, including effectiveness. Choices, not results, are presented as we go along. The alternatives may be interesting, repulsive, or neutral. We see what we can do with them. We make something of them; and, having done so, we may come to regret it. On the second concept, we wager that playing the game achieves results, not choices. We gamble only on our own adequacy to play the game. Which conception appeals to us depends on our estimate of the value of achieving the end result, the probabilities of doing so, and the costs of failure.

My point is that, except in high-tech vocational education, where she has become a tool, Alma Mater no longer presents a live option, and this in consequence of what has happened to the human self in contemporary societies. The songs in her praise embarrass her children; she has become, in their language, "irrelevant"—irrelevant to them, as they are. A multiform, disjointed society has made the self multiform and disjointed. A jungle of desires must be ordered. Class structures, religious faiths, dreams of dedication exist as much as ever, but assaulted, under revision, challenged. Selves not challenged to form themselves are not of this world. Alma Mater has ceased to be feasible except for those who have never known the exigencies of confusion and decision. In consequence, institutions of higher education will require of themselves and of others only a modest faith in their ability to know the welfare of their students and faculty, and make no bones about their ability to control the critical circumstances. Secular institutions, they conceive themselves in the service of those of little faith. From the point of view of those who run them, this ought to be something of a relief.

Now, assuming Alma Mater dead or moribund, why would anyone voluntarily embrace the processes of a higher education that presented itself as a kind of gambling house? Why would anyone want to assume the risks? After all, there is always the possibility of skipping higher education entirely, or of settling for the higher vocationalism most institutions make available.

First, one might be inclined to assume the risks because there is no avoiding some such risks in any case. There is no evidence that the working man is less distraught in the historical mill than others. There is no evidence that the securities manipulator has done himself much good beyond making money. One might avoid facing the risks—for example, by opting for institutions that offered salvation or growth. But, of course, to avoid facing a risk is not the same as avoiding the risk.

Next, the house of higher education expands the domain of choice beyond what one would have any likelihood of enjoying elsewhere. The reasoning is somewhat like that which favors leaving the small town for the big city. Higher education offers so many more opportunities that are on the whole far more interesting. As we say, one can make something of oneself. That is always an advantage, and it is all the greater when the resources for a variety of outcomes are carefully and deliberately presented.

Third, the spread of possibilities in terms of which one might make a life is not only larger, as in the big city; it includes possibilities of which society very much approves and which are integral to the civilization of that society. For a self constrained to form itself in a society, that is essential. Given some initial assurance of the respect of others, the individual gains the serious possibility of self-respect. Now new possibilities in terms of which one might make a life, new ways of building self-respect, emerge that might make one at least partly independent of market values. Gaining freedom in one's estimation of oneself is a substantial reason to assume the risks of fouling up.

A fourth reason for entering this particular gambling house of higher education is more troublesome. It raises the question of who you are to begin with. John Stuart Mill wondered why, in effect, one would rather be Socrates dissatisfied than Ronald Reagan satisfied. Obviously, not everyone would agree with that putative judgment. Mill thought that everything depended on whether one had experience of moral, intellectual, and aesthetic values as well as of those more generally shared. Like most others at the academy, I make the same assumption. People might justify themselves for accepting the risks of higher education because they find the payoffs of the gambling house more attractive than those of its alternatives. They value a civilized life, the involvement of the self in the complexities of an advanced civilization, even if the consequences do not make them wealthy or content. They feel that they, at least, have no choice.

Fifth, as pointed out before, the house is on the side of the players. The faculty who run the game and the students who play are not involved in a competition; they have the same positional interests. The participants may expect one another's help. They also have a right at least to expect the help of those who run the institution.

Sixth, the players have the right to assume that they just might break the bank and do so in virtue of their very failures. Out of dissonance and confusion might come the new insight, the new alternative, the new life of artist, scholar, person of action. Though the odds are never very good, the gains to the self-interested self may be enormous. It is rational to incur serious risks for very great ends.

Most people are aware of the seventh and last of my considerations in justification of gambling in higher education. Some are moved by it, though it seems so much less important, so much less serious than "making it" in a profession or "growing." Aside from the profit and the loss, there is the excitement of the extraordinary enterprises to which they may be invited. One undertakes the risks to the self and the uncertainty for adventure, wonder, fulfillment, novelty, fraternity, competition within the activity of the higher education, and for the sake of the gamble itself. The richness of the present experience itself justifies the game of higher education for those who play.[10]

So much for the general justification of higher education as a kind of gambling system. Plainly, much more can and, in a discussion of the choices of higher education, must be said. But, for the time being, the above may suffice if it is understood that none of it denies that there are students—and faculty—

who will take no chances beyond those they cannot avoid. They know what they want. For them anything they learn is only for use on the world; it makes no difference to *them* except for that. They work like Trojans, and the fact that they may be efficient at learning anything, including the subject matters of a classical education, proves only their determination to get ahead. So far as they are concerned, the only risk they will undertake lies in whether the bet they place on law, medicine, engineering, business, or a position teaching classics will succeed. Their only live positional interest is the interest in effectiveness.

Nevertheless, such individuals ought to remember that the assimilation of higher education to vocational or professional education does not exclude self-formative commitments. The self is not on one side with its life on the other. As everyone knows, professional educations too make certain kinds of people. "Making it," one also makes one's self. One does not escape the consequences of the choice, only the awareness.

But it is time now to turn directly to the choices of higher education. Given the positional interests, and preeminently the interest in self, given the thesis of sociality and the normal conditions of social incoherence, given the consequent trouble with growth, given the gambling system, the risks, the gains and uncertainty of the bets we place in higher education—given all this, what would a self-interested participant choose among the principal policy alternatives of higher education?

Chapter Four

The Relationships of Education

ONE OF THE ESSENTIAL CHOICES of higher education involves the kinds of relationships to be established between educated and educators in the educative process. They are relationships among persons in institutional roles insofar as they are constrained by those roles. The question is, which among the possible relationships satisfy the positional interests.

While students educate students, faculty faculty, and students faculty, these relations, however fruitful, are substantially unconstrained by the institutional rules and are left, for the most part, to personal preference and chance. One cannot claim to benefit from them in virtue of one's position as a faculty member or a student. I shall not pursue the interesting question whether they ought to remain this way or to be more or less formally incorporated within the structures of student and faculty roles.[1] The fact is that the educative process as it exists is built around the relationship of students and instructors; the nature of the relationship to be instituted among them is central among the policy choices of higher education.

These are the alternatives: either the educator works as a device for the student, the student becomes material for the educator to work, or an interaction occurs that resembles, as I shall suggest, a ballet or dance. People probably have the first two in mind when they construe the relationship of education as the relation of teacher and taught.

In the first relationship, instructors, like books and computers, have become tools for the self-instructing learner to employ; however much they talk to their students, they are not participants in the process. They may indeed seek to have it otherwise. But if they do—and of course they do not always—students may not let them. They may be excluded from the minds of those they address even when providing information that might answer questions—sometimes, indeed, precisely because they are understood to be doing just that. Students are self-taught, faculty conceived by students and themselves as, in the weary but significant expression, "textbooks wired for sound." It hardly matters if the professorial spiel is less than formal or if students can raise their hand instead of flipping to the index. Faculty are at bottom information providers.

No one need deny either the value of information providers for the self-instructor or the importance of self-instruction. Ultimately, every learner is an autodidact. But ultimately is always a long way off. In the meanwhile, before the final days, it matters that in this relationship of education the voice heard is overheard, that it lacks the power to enter unpredictably, on its own, for its own purposes, into another self's self-engagement. This only other agents can do—actual supporters, rejecters, appreciators, partisans, who, in refusing to accept the relationship of instrumentality, create with us the relationships in terms of which we may define where we stand. Instruments, however, even if human, while they may present puzzles and tasks, provide information, and test skills, leave only one participant. Students are deprived of a present context of active dialogue with those who have joined them in a common enterprise and share their ends.

It is, after all, helpful intellectually as well as morally not to be the center of the world. The consequences of autodidacticism are well known. Institutions of higher education that do not take them seriously in the conduct of educational affairs have, to that degree, failed the self-interest of their students. Faculty in such cases seek nothing more than to have their teaching load reduced.

The second relationship of education, in which students are material to be worked, does more than subject them to the instructor's demands. Authoritarian, it requires that they identify their own voice with the external voice heard and incorporate the witness of the authority as their own standard of judgment. Failure to do so becomes an irrefutable reason for self-condemnation. Education has transformed the individual into her own enemy, the disciplinarian for the authorized demand. To save itself the self surrenders itself. Pride becomes the first of the educational sins.

Still, while settling what one is to want through self-surrender has the virtue of simplicity, the method hardly accords with an interest in higher education that includes self-determination. While the instrumental relationship may have some limited value for students who, already knowing what they want, may be interested only in effectiveness, the authoritarian relationship has no redeeming value. Institutions which choose authoritarianism for the central relationship of education have turned against themselves as institutions of higher education.

One hastens to add the obvious caveat. The objection to an authoritarian education does not preclude respecting and making use of others' experience and insight. An authoritative and an authoritarian education are not the same. In the former, the learners grant only a presumption that instructors know whereof they speak. They must grant it, or there is no moving on. The authoritarian education, on the other hand, makes no distinction between a presumption (which may be withdrawn at any time) and a grant of belief in perpetuity.

Though the point is old hat, that does not render it less important. Granting a presumption does not interfere with the educative process. Students may still find in what instructors say pictures of the world and human beings they would do well to value. The difference is that they decide. The very possibility of withdrawal of the presumption, furthermore, makes available a way of differentiating and forming wants of particular importance for younger people determined to make something of themselves. Rebellion forms intellectual as well as personal character. In any field of inquiry, for persons of any age, true creativity will thrive as much on the final refusal to accept a presumption as on the original grant. Authoritarians, whether educators or students themselves, are the less suited for the processes of student self-interest for not acknowledging as much.

In the first possible relationship between educators and educated, then, students pretty much ignore instructors. In the second, instructors ignore the students' right to make their own choices. In the third—the relationship of primary concern here—the parties respond to one another as persons in shifting, developing, mutually adaptive patterns. They do not merely respect one another's "rights," whatever those rights might be; they deal with one another as other selves. The reciprocity of bodily movement that in dance converts movement into gesture is paralleled by a reciprocity of persons that converts talk into the complex movement of dialogue.

The precedent for the metaphor comes from the *Laws*. There, speaking of the choral dance as a vital part of education, Plato writes, "Through this sense [the power to enjoy rhythm and melody] [the gods] stir us to movements and become our choir leaders. They string us together on a thread of song and dance." [2]

There is more to the parallel with dance than group calisthenics. In higher education, too, through that reciprocity of developing selves, the members form themselves and one another, are strung together on a thread of process as dancers in the dance. They *are* dancers, the movement of each justified by the movement of the others. To be sure, in this dance, unlike Plato's, they dance in conflict as in synchrony. Their movements are not choreographed in advance. Still, they are bound together in their debates; their differences string them together. New words emerge, new lyrics, and hence future bindings. They are not the less affected in being strung together in disharmonies they struggle in common to resolve.

In the ballet of education, teacher and taught entangle themselves in each other's standpoint. That those who have called themselves educators deal with persons has been emphasized often enough. It is essential that the entanglement go the other way also, as the criticism of authoritarian relationships presumed. Students need, that is, to come to grips with faculty. They too need to push and probe. When they recognize this need, then students and faculty do and undo one another in a reciprocal performance. Who can be sure what the other side will say or do? The steps of each have meaning in relation to the steps of the other. Hence the sensitivity and the risk. There is no certainty in what one might say or think oneself. That's the point of the dance.

Accordingly, instructors bring to the education not a "method," however well-intentioned, of educating others; they bring themselves. They chance not merely the reformation of others but, in that process of reformation, the reformation of themselves in whatever ways pertain to their common enterprise. In primary and secondary education—and there is much of that in so-called higher education—educators may learn about the educated and maintain a high sensitivity to their needs and to their own conduct in relation to those needs. Still, so far as the subject is concerned, they have been there before; they lead the young where they want the young to go. Their destination is never in doubt. Only in higher education do educators learn what they think in the exploration of the subject matter.

Somehow, instructors seem to accept with equanimity the role of practitioners of a method; they are satisfied to *follow* a method. For the performance of set tasks, something of this sort may be desirable. But, in higher education at least, to accept the application of a method for the heart of the job is rather like confusing the technique of playing the violin with making music. Even those who strut their unmethodical hour before a class, puffing themselves up, putting themselves down, taking their pratfalls, at least bring themselves to bear. Awkward and laughable they may be; still, they take their business personally. Unlike the method follower whose self is prearranged, they deal as persons with persons. The images they present to others they present live; and the way others take those images affects those who offered them in the first place. Which is educated, which is educator? The dancers stumble, trip one another up. But even the failure of the performance testifies to an enterprise other than acquiring or transmitting information or techniques.

For those who do not know what to want, the ballet is the essential self-interested choice. Instructors must, and will, provide information and correction—the ballet could hardly proceed otherwise; but in the ballet their instrumental function is subordinated. The authoritative relationship (*not* the authoritarian) serves the essential function of providing a lead and focus to the reciprocity that must be at the heart of the dance of the self-interested. Still, the lead and focus are for a dance that remains open; they are there only to make the dance possible. For the purposes of self-formation, however, the ballet in which the dancers find their steps as they go, in response to the steps of others in the dance, alone of the relationships realizes the full potentiality of higher education. Because of that dance, the potentiality is, as has been intimated, that of a gambling system. The results of all the arguing and questioning in determining what one is to want become anybody's guess. Each participant is free, yet all are tied together.

It is a matter of some importance that the relationships of education outlined here hold for all the transactions of higher education, not just for those that occur in the classroom. The tutorial, for example, constitutes a powerful and often indispensable way of conducting those transactions, particularly at the more advanced levels; yet the tutorial is always one on one, not one on many as in the classroom. Indeed, the ballet takes place all the more effectively when the principals are face to face, while the authoritarian and manipulative modes of education are not less so because they occur one on one. Only a widespread sentimentalism that holds "personal" relations inevitably more desirable than impersonal ones makes it seem otherwise and so obscures the fact that in education, as elsewhere, people give and take the most fearful beatings close in on one another.

Some approach the relationships among faculty and students in very different terms than those employed here. Noticing the possibility of freedom and social bonding, they invoke, in order to establish what those relationships ought to be, not an image of a spontaneously choreographed dance but the relationships of persons in a democracy. Democracy is held to justify higher education and—if all goes as it ought—higher education presupposes democracy. On this view, the relationships of education are intrinsically democratic.

Literally, democracy means rule of the *demos*, of "the people." Rule of the people or the many is better in most cases than rule of the few. Having decided as much, students (and often faculty), rejecting authoritarian relationships in principle, may even extend their rejection to authoritative voices. In any event, where the relationships of education are conceived in terms of ruling and being ruled, self-interested persons, generalizing their experience, naturally select the principle of majority rule for the conduct of the business of education.

The problem with adopting the democratic model for the relationships of education is that to do so runs counter to the self-interest of the participants. For those who would adopt such a model think that what the voices of the participants do or do not count for equally is a governing process. They think, so fixed are the categories of domination and submission, that the government is the problem in education as elsewhere. Yet given a choice between being governed by others, even democratically by a majority of others, and not being governed by anyone else, any self-interested party will choose the latter. If the ballet is a legitimate mode of relationship in education, then higher education has such a choice. All relationships of government may be and ought to be put aside in favor of the cooperation of each and every participant in the achievement of the participant's own goals as fixed by positional interests. In short, the self-interested relationship of education is more like friendship than democracy, even though, unlike personal friendship, it constrains the relationship among the participants in a particular context and in relation to specific interests. Higher education is one of the few institutional areas of modern life that might aim at friendship in virtue of the nature of its process.

In rejecting the rule either of the many or of the one for the relationships of education, I in no way propose some form of the radical individualism that often characterizes students in institutions of higher education. The rule of radical individualism represents not friendship but the fracturing of rule—each individual his own polity. Individuals rule themselves for themselves, seek an advantage over other students through examinations and the control of the instructor's judgment. They have become competitors.

Competitors, even if not necessarily enemies, are not friends to one another or to those they use to their advantage. They are on their own. They may or may not care much for what they are doing; their ranking in what they are doing is all. They gamble not themselves but what they may or may not get, and turn their instructors into instruments for improving their intellectual capital. They have become the academic analogue of the free market entrepreneur. So, where the political paradigm underlay the conception of the relationships of education in terms of democracy versus autocracy, the acquisitive econ-omy now receives a free translation within higher education. Self-rule substitutes for the dance.

Yet if there exists a particular domain in which the participa-tion of each, even in the competitions of that domain, is to the advantage of each in securing his or her own interest, that will surely be preferred to one in which that is not the case. If indi-viduals have indeed the positional interests claimed for them in higher education, that domain does exist. Their relation to one another in their pursuit of their interest as students and faculty is cooperative in virtue of the competition, competitive in virtue of the cooperation. It is a complex relationship that I must now seek to describe.

Chapter Five

The Ballet of Higher Education

To see how the complex relationship of the ballet might exist and form the self through the transforming of its wants, we turn to the characteristic features of that relationship: style, where the impact on self is most immediately felt; theme, which sets the domain of higher education; and the qualifications for participating in the dance.

Style, our way of being whatever it is we are, constitutes a prime concern of the interest in self-formation. Style in the pursuit of the themes of higher education presupposes methods, techniques, information, theories, as much as does the achievement of effectiveness in the world. But methods, techniques, and so on are not as such style. In acquiring them, we turn outward to the field of action; we are interested, perhaps, for the sake of the self but not therefore in the self. We show style in the way we employ them. Hence style, unlike effectiveness, is never the product of a set of instructions. Though other people's style may be presented before us, so many valuable possibilities for our working, our own is a consequence of the interrelationships of persons in the dynamic system called here the ballet. So, for example, the methods required for work in physics would impose constraints on the participants in the form of scientific methods. Those "methods" are learned in the course of the ballet. Still, nobody does science by prescription; no one, literally, "applies" scientific method. Doing science requires employing that method in a certain way; and at this point one thinks of rigor, imaginativeness, willfulness, unconventionality, daring, all of which are lived into, are made—if education is successful—in the educational ballet. Such characteristics of attitude and action, taken collectively, I have called "style."

Styles vary, of course, with the domain of thought and action in which they occur. More essentially, not all are necessarily good or desirable. Clarity of expression, wit, grace, delicacy of touch, rigor, have their opposites. Obscurity, dullness, awkwardness, heavy-handedness, sloppiness also constitute styles, bad styles. Failures rooted in the self, they also come about through an interplay of persons that includes the interplay of the self with itself. Good or bad, however, the style belongs to individuals; it characterizes them to one another and to themselves.

So qualities of style are not incidental, as the single-minded concentration on the curriculum and its teaching implies. They are of the essence for the student and professor interested in the enactments of their relations to the other; they are what each in the relationship will tend most to remember and preserve. They are manifested where literature, art, and science present unique opportunities for their development, expression, and reinforcement; they become palpable when great stylists through their works enter into and mold the relationship between students and teachers.

In higher education, as elsewhere, substance is often set off against style, just as results (as the pragmatist complains) are set off against process, possession against use, ends against means. One looks to the bottom line and, for the sake of the return on life, rejects the quality of the life. Confusing style with the absence of substance, naturally enough one finds it vacuous and pretentious.

Many in the university situation take this point of view. Conceiving their function in terms of a no-nonsense professionalism, they fail to see that that point of view turns students and instructors into anonymous instruments for their own or other people's ambitions. Aspiring only to perform their function, they objectify and leave small room for wit, grace, or delicacy. They are sincere; the subject is all. They fear above all the con man. When they study style, if they do, they treat it as an observed phenomenon, from the outside. They have become minimalists. Rejecting style, they unwittingly develop another kind of style. They have made a choice of educations that calls for the ignoring of the perceived quality of themselves as selves and hence of other selves as selves. The interest in the self is crippled.

The alternative, minimalists suppose, must be imitation. For them, people who show style provoke the question of whom they think they're imitating. To be sure, minimalists are right to think poorly of imitators. They think of them as pretenders. Still, the persistence of style in education or anywhere else hardly demands reducing live selves to copies, even first-rate copies. Wearing a mask, even one's own, marks the end of style except for the style of wearing a mask—a thin and wearing affair unless one is in a Greek tragedy or playing games. For wearing masks as such is hiding. The styling of the ballet does not hide; it uses, takes off from, relates.

Those who do the fine arts present the model for a styling that does not mask. For them the art of others is the starting point. No art of others, no art. Artists doing their art make use of what they have found about them; and that, more than subject matter, is the manner and quality called style. But finding that styles do or do not work, they change them, build upon them, until perhaps new styles arise. Such a possibility the ballet of education presents for its participants. Imitation is prologue.

With a self to be formed, no self-interested person would have it differently.

Other occasions will arise to consider the particular relevance of the arts for higher education. For now, it is not trivial to note that style, in higher education as in the arts, entails more than an interchange among those physically present. Heard also in the interchange, loud and clear, are the voices of absent presences. Provided only that it not be held against people that they are dead, they enter into the exchange between master and apprentice, instructor and student. Questioned, added to, denied, they must be heard in the discussions of the arts and sciences or there is no significant exchange, let alone a question of style.

The second characteristic element of the educational ballet is theme. The dances of the ballet—the different kinds of dances in the repertory will be dealt with later—have themes or sets of themes in virtue of which the dancers relate to one another and the dance exists. One speaks of a "theme" in order to describe what is to be done with or about a subject matter or activity. Courses or sections of courses not constructed around themes are meaningless. Groups of courses justify themselves by the theme or themes that run through them. Curricula search for a theme.

The same subject matter may admit of many themes. To the degree one formulates it, a theme is a theory for the organization of the materials; as such, it sets the terms for the complex relationships among the participants in the dance. I use the term "theory" not in the sense of a general predictive hypothesis or set of hypotheses but in the sense of a vision of how materials—propositions, works of art and sets of them, historical events, social institutions—fit together and acquire meaning in that fitting together. The specific purpose of the educational ballet is to work up and develop the theme.

That the relationship of higher education revolves around themes that students grasp rather than subject matters that they "learn" is essential. Subject matters are given. Take them or leave them. There is no occasion for the dance. Themes are another matter. They are altered, expanded, re-created in terms of the development of the relationship among the participants, given an initial statement of the theme. Absent a theme, though the subject matter remains, the ballet ceases; the participants in the dance, having lost their context of interaction, have lost the dance.

The French Revolution is not as such a theme but a reference. If one studies the French Revolution in the sense of higher education, one seeks a theme in terms of which to understand—indeed, to make judgments about—the events that occurred and to determine in what sense they occurred, if they did. The theme—depending on how one regards the French Revolution—might be the development of democracy or the perspectives of the totalitarian state.

Which, now, are the themes of the ballets or transactions of higher education? The formation of the "mind" or "intellect" of the individual, and to that extent the formation of the self of the individual, will, of course, depend on them. Their subject matter may or may not be "intellectual"; if it were only that, most human life would drop out of higher education, as people often suppose to be the case. The themes of higher education are, simply, those that emerge in the arts, the sciences, high technology, the social sciences, and history when the possibilities of human intelligence and sensitivity are pressed. An institutional approach to the choices of higher education demands that much. That at the same time considerable disagreement may arise over just which are the developed civilizations, just which exhibit intelligence and sensitivity in the highest degree, and hence what the proper themes are for course and curricula, is to be expected. The search for the theme is part of higher education. That education which regards themes as fixed will have guaranteed itself permanent irrelevance to the arts, sciences, technology, and the concerns of higher education in general.

I do not presume to settle differences over the proper themes of higher education. Nevertheless, from the institutional point of view, relevant constraints on any settlement are discernible. Above all, disagreements will be managed, or a significant effort made to manage them, by appeal to a shared ground of knowledge, experience, and value. This means, in the language of C. S. Peirce, that the attempt to determine in what higher education consists will occur not through tenacity, authority, or a priori definitions, but through method that in its own terms distinguishes a right from a wrong way and makes progressive and controlled controversy possible.[1] It also means that in the argument over what falls into relevant culture and civilization due weight will be given to the range of practices at institutions of higher education. "Due weight" signifies that, while those practices are subject to change, they set the agenda of the discussion. The burden of proof falls upon those who would substitute other agenda than those in use for the culture and civilization in which the institution exists.[2]

Let us, for the sake of discussion, assume the boundaries of culture and civilization determined and the appropriate themes instituted. How, broadly, do the themes of the sciences, literature, philosophy, social science, and so on affect the interest of the participants in their self-formation? That they do is less immediately obvious than that style does; for style is grasped as an immediate aspect of the personality.

From the themes chosen in the ballet come constraints on admissible styles. Different dances call for different styles. Indeed, to develop style in the deeper sense requires sensitivity toward the differing stylistic requirements of different dances. So themes that differentiate the dances count to those for whom style or address toward the world and themselves matter. Each student and participant in higher education comes to recognize both that one may style the same cat in more than one way and that some cats will not style the way one likes. Themes encountered, themes worked up, shape the styles that together define the person's way of living in the culture.

The effect of themes upon the formation of the self and its wants, however, goes further than style. Themes grasped define "minds." Minds are selves defined in relation to the interests of a civilization. The business of the choice of themes is to form minds, along with opportunities for styles of mind, and, therefore, at least to the extent that the nature of our minds determines what we shall want, selves. Selves constructed in relation to the themes of higher education are, of course, hardly equivalent to the selves confronted in early morning wakefulness or psychiatry. Placement in relation to the themes and their development is the issue. Placed in a different world, we see ourselves differently; we identify ourselves differently. We are, as it is said, civilized people; we exist in the life of the culture, and partly through the themes consider and evolve the norms to guide our choices.

Of course it is the theme *in the ballet* that affects the self, not the theme as such. In itself, stated and observed, a characteristic of events, it is merely duly noted. As the theme of the ballet's moving interrelationships, it becomes a kind of potency for persons to bring to bear beyond the specific subject matter that it organizes. The theme comes to re-form other subject matters with different variations. Played again—danced again— with different emphases, it acquires different meaning, extends different meanings. A theme for the French Revolution extends beyond the French Revolution. It is manifested, shaped, in that revolution but not coterminous with it. It pertains, therefore, to the possible futures, in the educative process and out, of those who apprehend it. Linked up with other themes, it goes to form a mind.

Some cautionary underlinings are in order. First, no one can grasp the theme of the ballet, or get the drift of a course of study, without tracing the specifics. Without them, themes become gas, shibboleths to show membership in some favored group. Also, we may sometimes acquire the specifics and, missing the theme, never perceive their point. Then, no matter how serious the material remembered, it is remembered trivially. It means, precisely, as people say, nothing to them, since they have no reason in the nature of what they know to know it. *They* have no reason; *they* have nothing to gain. Having got the theme, however, they have got a disposition for acquiring and using certain kinds of specifics. Educators must give up the vanity of expecting that much detail will or, indeed, should be remembered.

Next, and harder still, educators must surrender even the more modest expectation that all or most of the students who do their duty in higher education will grasp every theme they encounter. If even their instructors cannot, why should they? Not only human limitations make the idea absurd. The fact is that not all dances are compatible. The possibility of dis-preparation, of foreclosure of some alternatives in the process of realizing others, is a condition of the enterprise. To succeed in grasping a style appropriate to the development of some theme, may sometimes—depending on the theme, the individual and the circumstances—ruin the person for another style, another theme. We don't have infinite minds. Some have supposed this to mean merely that we lack all the information we need to grasp the theme. But information is eventually manageable. Hook up with a supercomputer. The trouble lies elsewhere. We can't handle all themes.

We consider now who is qualified for the dance, given its themes and styles.

In identifying the dancers, it is expedient at the outset to put aside some obvious misconceptions. Privilege does not qualify anyone. Neither, at the same time, does deprivation justify participation by the desperate of the world. Cultivated accents are not qualifications, nor money, nor sex, nor race, nor the experience of injustice.

Neither, we may add, do the offices of deans, presidents, and other administrative statesmen qualify them as teachers writ large. Their function is instrumental, their business to rent the hall, assemble the cast, manage the budget, and in general spare the participants their statesmanship. For necessary as they may be to the activity of higher education, they are not the educators they often consider themselves and the community outside the academy encourages them to believe. The mutuality, the reciprocity of the actual process, the themes, the styles, all lie outside their conceivable sphere. Their proper role is not rulership but the rule of henpeckery: bold as a lion abroad in society, fearful in the extreme at home, and conciliatory. Choreography is not their business.

This much understood, we turn to the question of the qualities proposed for the members of the dance in the ballet of higher education. The question is essential. In the formal ballet of the stage, one distinguishes Petrouchka from the dancer who performs Petrouchka—the dancer does a better or worse job. But in the ballet of higher education, the nature of the dancers determines not only the worth of a specific performance but the nature of the dance itself. The dancers and their distinguishing characteristics must be understood if one is to understand the very action of the ballet. The dance is a function of the dancers, not the dancers of the dance.

Minds, many would say, are the participants in any process of higher education. By minds they do not mean "selves defined in relation to the interests of a civilization." For them, minds are not outcomes but agents. Minds, according to their view, apprehend truths; minds learn to solve problems making use of those truths. The proper participants in higher education are for them, to use a favorite locution of Bloom, the "knowers."[3] Individuals enter the dance of higher education in virtue of a purely mental function. They observe and they register. They do not know Solomonically, as Solomon knew Sheba, and Sheba Solomon. They are, finally, voyeurs, even when they have to work to position themselves properly before the keyhole. Observers, however hard they work, don't dance. The self and its wants remain untouched. The issues are in the world. If one has a taste for that sort of thing, one watches how they arise and pass away.

Those who enter fully into the social and political issues of their time might think activists the dancers of choice. Activists look to higher education to prepare them to fight more effectively for what they have already decided is true and just. Activists do not, until their activism collapses under the weight of circumstances, normally question who they are or what they want. They know. The basic problems of self-formation no more occupy the center of their field of consciousness than they do the minds of the knowers. To achieve a special kind of effectiveness, they will sacrifice anything. In consequence, activists, like knowers, have no essential need for the dance. The dance merely sharpens their skills.

The educational transaction, another story goes, does not, like most social transactions, aim to satisfy persons in specific and limited respects; it does anything it very well can to satisfy individual students as they are. The relationship of education, on this view, approaches all-purpose philanthropy; it seeks, within the limits of practicality, to supply whatever the individual needs to be happy. The ballet here is the ballet of helping, the teacher the helper, the student the helped. The teacher's moves aim primarily to encourage student self-expression. The not infrequent consequence is to intensify the individual's puzzlement and isolation. For just whom is this self to be expressed? What does it want? What would express it? Student and faculty sentimentalism runs rampant. Off the institution goes, losing whatever direction it had in its quest to satisfy an unsatisfiable market.

If the members of the ballet participate neither as pure brains nor as would-be activists nor as the self-involved, who and what are they? In general, of course, they must be those who see and form themselves in relation to the themes and styles of civilization that they at the same time test, form, and re-form through a common enterprise and a common interchange. Yet the question remains just who those are. For many, the ballet I have been describing is not a live option. They lack either the required intellectual ability or the temperament for the involvement of their passions, tastes, expectations in the culture of a civilization. The social transaction of educator and educated reduces either to a matter of brains and puzzles, feelings and self-expressions, or politics. From our point of view, the agents in such a transaction are outside the dance. Their full interest as participants is never touched. Their contribution to the educative process may be useful; those who learn their lessons are paid in full with high grades and entry into medical school. But they remain supernumeraries.

The qualifying characteristics of those prepared to assume their place in the choral dance include, of course, the ones for which many institutions routinely try to test—brains, skills, talents, knowledge that might be brought to bear, critical attitudes, inventiveness, willingness to learn. Enough has been said about them. I have nothing to add. If, however, as I have argued, institutions of higher education presuppose not growth as their operative aim but the provision of certain kinds of gambles, some other qualifying characteristics emerge.

The most obvious of these consists in the capacity to endure risk and uncertainty while taking pleasure in the process that creates them.[4] In this respect the process matches only imperfectly the art of the dance. There, to be sure, someone might slip, the dance might not come off. But there the ends are known, the steps choreographed. In the ballet of higher education, one does not know the norms in advance; they are sought, worked on, worked through in the dance. The steps, except in the most obvious mechanical way ("Read such and such first, then such and such, then we'll talk about it"), cannot be choreographed. The whole point is in the not knowing, in the exploration, in the gamble that something surprising might turn up.

Not all temperaments can take that. Some students must

know exactly where they are and why. Some faculty must block out their contribution in advance. Both abort the process of education as ballet. For they cannot extemporize in the moving interchange of their responses. They do not educate one another; they do not form themselves. They move data back and forth.

Malleability conjoined with a certain hardness of character and mind also characterizes proper participants in the dance if they are to change one another and in the process be changed. If they cannot resist, they cannot change others; they lack the strength. If they cannot change others, they cannot be changed; they lack the occasion. Educators, thinking of their charges, like to identify educability with malleability. That is sheer arrogance. Education is not imprinting. There is no interplay without prejudice, without the willingness to move on an uncertainty. None do well without confidence strong enough to move others and allow themselves to be moved. The stubborn and humble, the contentious and open, the self-contradicted, are the right ones for the dance.

All this involved instructors know about their students though not necessarily about themselves. They, too, must be able both to yield and to overcome and grant that right to their students, or there is no dance. Our dancers, faculty and students alike, become competitors who need one another. They compete with themselves as with others. They are equipped to acknowledge both gain and loss. They form combinations and oppositions; they shift sides; they cooperate and oppose. In this way, within the context of higher education, they learn what they are to want. Such I take to be the moral of the Socratic dialectic for higher education. Protagoras questions Socrates, Socrates Protagoras; each finally must question himself. That is how values are formed and re-formed.

Those qualified for the ballet must be capable, finally, of accepting the constraint of respect. I do not mean just that respect for the rights of others expected anywhere, but respect for the particularity of persons in the exchanges of the dance. Failure in respect terminates the relationship of education. Individuals denied this respect, the objects of contempt however polite, are worked on, or for, or against rather than treated as fellow dancers to whose objectives one accommodates in the common concern. That accommodation, that respect for fellow dancers in the ballet, implies consideration for the life of persons as they are when encountered in the interplay. By accepting the legitimacy of backgrounds, perspectives, dreams, and intentions not one's own, perhaps alien, perhaps distorting, one can know what moves to make. It is just the need of this grant of respect that makes the ballet of education so fragile and the dancer's capacity to accord it so essential.

Respect implies, of course, attending also to the particularity of those others who do not physically appear. Taking the voice of the most ancient writer out of its own context so far as that context can be determined vitiates the constraint of respect as much as taking the voice of instructor or student out of the context in which he or she has spoken. If anyone inquires why we simply do not use the old documents as reading them makes us think of them, and never mind the writer's context, there is a ready response: we might with equal reason use the voices of those we hear not as voices of others but as voices heard in our private dream. Sometimes there are advantages. But to the extent we do this, we lose the force of novelty and opposition; the ballet of higher education has expired, forfeit to the loss of what I have called respect.

At the end of Chapter 4 I suggested that the cooperative, competitive relationship among the participants in the educative process as they pursued the same interests was more like friendship than rule. Now we have, in virtue of the educational ballet's characteristic concern with style and theme and of the qualifications demanded of its performers, including mutual respect, essayed to fix upon the special life that might be lived in higher education so close to friendship. And I have proposed that the furtherance of that life would be the alternative of choice at any institution concerned with the welfare of its people.

We must now go on to the other major policy choices that institutions of higher education face if they propose to meet the positional interests of their participants.

Chapter Six

General Education

HIGHER EDUCATION AT THE university includes a "general" education, the "liberal" education of which the general is a part, and professional and graduate educations. What might self-interested participants legitimately expect of the courses of study that go under those labels? I ask this first for general education.

Though sometimes used as the equivalent of liberal education, the expression frequently refers to the education intended primarily for the first portion of the academic career of most undergraduates. Undergraduates are supposed to acquire that information of the arts and sciences expected of anyone who has had a higher education, rather as the entire population is supposed to acquire the information necessary to function fully in the community. A general education, then, attempts to provide what E. D. Hirsch calls "cultural literacy"—"the basic information necessary to thrive in the modern world," "the network of information a competent reader possesses"—to a degree and of a sort beyond the reach of secondary schools.[1] Such knowledge it calls "general." In effect, some people are to be more literate than others.

If, however, cultural literacy on one level or another is the object, problems naturally arise in setting the requirements of literacy. For primary and secondary schools, where the requirements may be set at ground level, the way is relatively clear.

Even though problems enough remain in setting a ground level for very different sorts of people, practical agreement will often be readily attainable. There are some things probably everybody ought to know and some things everybody ought to be able to do or heaven help them. Disagreements exist at the not insignificant penumbra.[2] For higher education, on the other hand, the problem is more acute; its participants both share any general need for "literacy" and, as participants in higher education, are presumed to experience a further requirement. What should any one of *them* be expected to be able to "read"?[3] If we are thinking of what shared knowledge would be required as a base to build upon, what are they supposed to build to?

Rather than responding directly to these questions, most faculties establish courses presenting the essential structure of the various disciplines and their subject matters. Students are to find what they need to know in prescribed survey courses. The courses, selected after considerable competition among the disciplines, communicate (supposedly) what seems to their preparers, after the summing and subtracting of their innumerable preferences, to be demanded not by them but by the discipline under the tight constraints of limited time and limited student capacities. This, of course, results in perpetually dissatisfied faculty who would like to see more and more in the course. (They know their discipline is endlessly demanding and they have their standards.) Bored students try to avoid the course or get it over with in a hurry.

I do not deny that very often perfectly reasonable judgments are made on what out there on the spreadsheet of culture ought to go into a general education. Still less do I intend to enter the argument about whether "facts" are to be accumulated or "skills" learned in the acquirement of cultural literacy. Information and ways of using information, verification and theory, the nature of problems and ways of resolving them, are too interdependent to make a discussion in terms of skill versus fact in education very helpful. I propose instead to consider a general education as the product of the disciplines *plus* the nature, prospects, and choices of the persons to whom the education applies. If committees employed that second consideration more often than pure scholarship concedes, survey courses might begin to become defensible. That does not help very much in composing lists of things every college sophomore ought to know; but then, it is not supposed to. For the self-interest of the students is the issue, not the satisfaction of customary expectations of what an otherwise undefined educated person should know.

What in a general education satisfies the student self-interest is, generally, this: whatever the preferences—whatever specific content the individual in his or her situation gives to the positional interests—each has an interest in seeing those preferences realizable in the social world. For that is where dispositions and inclinations become, precisely, interests. Hence all have an interest in the possible milieus in which they might be called upon to nurture their interests. A general education is, from the self-interested point of view, the precaution higher education offers against catastrophe; it attempts to limit the uncertainty under which people will make their decisions in the course of their studies and thereafter. In this sense, it provides an initial insurance against ineffectiveness and incoherence in both education and life, and therefore some provisional insurance against certain palpable kinds of injury to the interest in self.

It seems clear, then, that for such protection all would seek what I shall call maps. Maps of the social and cultural terrain and map reading are what students have a right to expect in the first phase of higher education, maps that locate possible places to visit or reside in, the relation of these places to one another, and how one might get to those places. Maps don't say where to go. For whatever reasons, you decide that after looking at them. That, too, is how social maps work. Hence the general conditions for effectiveness justify the employment of the maps of general education.

Survey courses, like maps of general education that fulfill their function, purport to trace the outlines of their worlds. There, however, the resemblance ends. The survey course bears no legend to relate it to any world; the possible relationship of the survey to those who take the course remains an unexamined mystery, and the requirements of effectiveness are missed. The map has ceased to be a map. That is why students object to survey courses—not because they are sketchy (that might merely mean less work), but because they do not know what the stuff might have to do with them. Surveys, as the stringing together of items every educated person ought to know, are, finally, samplings—fair samples, at best. Relations among those samplings are themselves sampled. But students in search of their own destination need more than samples. They need maps devised for their purposes.

Like physical maps, the social maps of a general education depict the characteristics of their terrain from a standpoint selected or assumed. That the education is general does not obviate the choice of a standpoint. No one would argue, on the grounds of generality, that the mapping requirements of college students are identical with those of elementary or high school students. Plainly, college students have, besides additional requirements of detail, requirements of complexity and kind. The class of persons for whom generality is of value must clearly be specified before the generality of a general education—or the "literacy" required of them—becomes meaningful. Only then can one begin to map out the possible terrains their users might explore.

How to identify the map users in a higher education is a question less remote and abstract than may at first appear. In deference more, perhaps, to practical necessity than to a judgment of educational wisdom, different classes of persons are in fact recognized, and what is presented is shaped to their requirements. Engineering or business schools will often have general programs for the people in their divisions quite different from the programs of liberal arts institutions. The point, however, is not that they will have "general" educations in the sense of establishing the literacy requirement for engineering or business; it is that what is requisite or fitting outside that literacy requirement for doing engineering or business—or medicine or law—will vary. Emphases will fall differently; the map will be more detailed in one area than another. And that is not simply the discretion that is the better part of valor but what makes the project worthwhile to those who find themselves in a certain position within the institution with certain expectations of what they will be doing in the world.

The problem of the nature of the general standpoint has still another dimension when one considers what the standpoints represented at the university might have in common. At the same time that there is a plurality of standpoints, people who belong to an institution of higher education belong to a certain class of persons. They are those, whatever their origins or social status, who are assumed to have, and assume themselves to have, the likelihood of a certain kind of participation in the society they are entering. They are supposed to be those who take the lead in the more complex and central activities of the society. That implies a wider field of awareness of consequences and relationships than the field required for other forms of participation. From this point of view, the different generalities in the general education begin to intersect and the points of intersection make possible reflections on "general" education at a university as though the generality were unqualified by reference to a class of persons.

There are, in brief, shared expectations. But where they are, what they are, and how significant they are now generates the major problem of defining the society in respect of which education will be general. This is the point at which fundamental splits, real or imagined, in the constitution and future of society create major differences over what a course ought to include or what courses are to be presented.

I leave it at that. A divided society will never permit complete agreement on the contents of a general education; it will paper over differences and substitute survey courses sketched from the perspective of absolute generality. I presuppose only that a common standpoint shared by those who engage in the profession and other major or minor leadership roles in society determines a commonality in the shape and structure of general education at the university. Differences in the representation of that shape and structure among the professions and other relevant roles are left to the separate faculties. But, given where the common expectations of persons in the roles of the university lie, these are the main terrains in which the construction of initial maps serves the "general" self-interest.

All, presumably, will need to know the overall structure of the society in which they function and expect to function. That is the primary terrain to be explored, normally through studies in history and the social sciences. All will want to conduct such an exploration in order to reduce the gross chances of disaster in patterning lives, as has already been stressed, but also to estimate the probability of the gains for which they might hope. Hence they will need to know not only the lay of the land as it is but the social causes and tendencies that make reasonable surmises of the future possible. So far we are like people concerned to inquire into a market for the sake of a good investment. What would we need to know? Where will we invest? "Surveys" of the social terrain advanced to answer parallel questions will be selected, constructed, and conducted differently from those that are not.

But the mapping of society has a utility for effectiveness that the stock market analogy misses. While the problem of achieving effectiveness certainly includes learning to adapt to the world as it is, that by no means eliminates the problem. The world may be changed, the conditions for effective behavior altered to the individual's advantage. There, in the peculiarly human relation to an environment, lies strong effectiveness— the big career—in any domain. To chart, in however preparatory a way, the possibility of new configurations in the social organization must be to the self-interest of anyone wishing to become an effective and integrated human being.

The usual assumption that a general education in the nature of the social order exists as preparation for assuming the responsibilities of citizenship goes only a short way toward "strong" effectiveness. "Good citizenship" principally implies learning how things are in order to support the existing social and political framework, and that means accepting the general conditions for effective participation in society. Accepting them, however, does not necessarily advance the interest of the individual, or the class to which the person belongs, or the society, or humanity in general. It is the blindest complacency to assume that a well-educated individual has to cherish the present order. Revolution, or reform, or simply cultivating one's own garden, might be as incumbent on the individual as "good citizenship." One would need a sense of the kind of action that might be required to achieve any of these. A general education might present the first intimations.

Not even the service of democracy is an appropriate end for a general education in social change and structure. Even if the idea of democracy were completely clear, a democracy for the purposes of education constitutes a prospect to be apprehended and assessed, not a dogma for the sake of which to cull the world for the supporting facts.[4] Many possible outcomes are charted on the maps that bear the name Democracy. What goes to make education "higher" and general education a legitimate part of it is the critique of institutions and their justifications. *Non serviam* is the only motto for a general education that serves the interests of the self.

So it appears that the most serviceable objective of a general education, even more than a precise map of the social terrain, will consist in the instituting of habits of reasonable criticism of the social milieu. Such criticism, grounded on the scrutiny of hypotheses and materials actually available, need make no impossible demands upon accuracy or create undue anxiety about covering the field. The consequences of a failure to make the best choice of hypotheses and materials will have been in some measure alleviated if address, sensitivity, and judgment in future circumstances can be increased—if, in effect, students learn how to make use of social mappings and how to expose those mappings themselves to criticism.

A comment now on the next mapping that seems appropriate to a general education: history. A broader study of history may serve as the antidote for the traditional ideal of civics. The discovery of other social worlds—worlds, in the bargain, that precede and pass into one's own—may both clarify one's own in the difference and the continuity and make alternatives conceivable. Hence criticism of present conditions becomes the more possible and history "relevant."

More deeply, perhaps, history may extend the community in which we exist. *This* past, as we say, is ours; it belongs to us. *This* happening, long past, has special relevance in giving definition to our lives and interests. The relevant community in which we exist as social selves expands and with it the possibilities of self-definition. Not only, therefore, is it sheer prejudice to hold it against other people that they are dead, it is self-defeating also when the forms and urgencies of actual past lives provide edge and outline to one's own, and one's life and interests find meaning in the connections. In this manner, the mapping of history passes beyond its utility for strong effectiveness and serves directly the interest in self-formation.

The third of the broad mappings that the practice of general education has established would of course have to be the education in the sciences, technology, art, literature of the culture. Even the sketchiest map of the social order and its history must in some measure deal with those subjects. But they must be grasped and dealt with, though summarily, not merely in relation to social contexts but in their own terms, as the usual courses in science survey, literature, and now, increasingly, computer technology and mathematics attest. One glimpses the materials in the context of the domain—the problems, the methods, how they have been answered, the successes, the failures. Pursuing the arts and sciences in something like their own terms may look like taking general education to provide introductory courses in the field. But while something of later use might well be acquired, that result is not the end of a general education, as most science curricula tend to confirm. (Science departments supply their own introductory courses specifically designed to provide a foundation on which to build and discharge any general education obligations with courses like "Physics for Poets" for which their faculties have only a limited respect.)

What, then, might justify for the self-interested the mappings of a general education in the various domains of the culture? First, self-interest requires, in order to know whether to bother entering on those domains, a basis on which to recognize what belongs to the domain and what does not. Listings of what belongs and what does not will not do; the discipline exists live only because any listing is incomplete. General education provides the basis for recognition. The idea is to be able to distinguish that which is on the map of the domain from that which is not. The assumption is that there are family resemblances in any of the fields in which general education works. If the things called physics have nothing in common in the complex way of family resemblances, there is no physics; if no family resemblances in literature, there is no literature. A sense of what is held in common provides the first basis on which to distinguish the real from the fake.

This does not imply that in concerning itself with recognition, general education generalizes. Formulating generalizations about the nature of physics or literature is a concern of philosophers, physicists, and critics. Generalizations, to be sure, may be helpful or harmful in focusing attention. Recognition, however, is not a matter of definition; it precedes, and justifies, the definition that may perhaps clarify it. "That is music; the other is noise." "That is physics; that is science fiction." "That is poetry;

this is nonsense." Obviously, we may change our judgments; but unless we begin with some sense of music or physics or poetry, of what has gone into them, we are in no position to make a judgment of any kind, even for ourselves. We need an intuitive basis for recognition. We get that by recognizing that the things encountered do or do not bear resemblances to those already discovered on the maps of the culture. We have seen members of the family before. They have been pointed out to us on the maps of a general education.

But what does it mean to have *seen* members of the family before? It means, for the elements of the culture, more than having had them pointed at and classified. One recognizes them for having worked with them. It is too much to expect the students of a general education to do physics, or poetry, or music, at the cutting edge. If they did, that would be the best of bases for recognition. But there is a plausible second best at which they might aim, a preparatory recognition that precedes the deeper kind; and general education may provide it. When it does, students get their noses rubbed in prime instances in the field; they see how people reached their conclusions, observe the logic. They notice how artists and scientists have gone about their art, notice how they used their predecessors. They see how poems work. Instead of absorbing catalogs of information about objects, students experience the object. Experienced, rather than reported, it appears on a map in a way that signifies. Under the guidance of the instructor, they have taken a first step toward recognizing the features on the ground that the map designated. They can "read" the map; the map has a semantical dimension.

In general education, whatever the art or science might come to mean ultimately in the life of individuals, the focus of attention falls outside the self and on the disciplines in which they might conceivably lose themselves. It is the focus only that falls there, however. While individuals are now not directly concerned with what they want or are to want but with the spread of possibilities, still, there is more to the exploration of the cultural map than mapping. Under the right circumstances, there is pleasure in those preliminary explorations beyond the satisfaction of having learned the score. Fascinating things have been encountered. The value of the happy encounter consists not only in itself or in the confirmation it provides of the good sense of studying further; it consists in the evidence it offers to persons seeking to form themselves that to exist as participating selves in a certain world, however modestly, suits them. They may, in a small measure, begin, as people say, "to find themselves" as civilized human beings; they have found that without necessarily making a career of the arts or sciences they go for them. The experience may in some undetermined measure shape their sympathies and sensitivities in their future lives.

The mapping of the arts, sciences, and technology in their own terms, then, differs for self-interested people in some respects from the mapping of the world of social involvements. In the world of social involvements, the map is preeminently a tool. In the world of the arts and sciences, the very pleasure that one may be led to take in an activity may introduce one to new possibilities for becoming oneself regardless of what comes of it in the daily business of life. One has been presented with a first, a provisional choice of what sort of self one will become, what one's wants and desires will be like in respects one has perhaps learned may be fundamental.

For present purposes we have dealt sufficiently with the nature of general education for the self-interested in the social, historical, and, broadly, intellectual domains. Institutions of higher education, in satisfying their commitment to the effectiveness of their students, will seek to institute a general education offering maps of the disciplines relevant to the class of individuals for whom the education is to be general; they will not assume that in a general education all undergraduates are in all respects alike. At the same time, they will not be content with maps that merely trace things as they are from the point of view of the student's interest in making out in the world as it is. The offered maps will provide, along with a quick glimpse of the products of the various disciplines, first intuitions of how those products came to be. Institutions of higher education will also further the interest in "strong" effectiveness by mapping possibilities for changes in the ordering of the social world. In such basic ways as these, students can be led to recognize their worlds in possible relationship to themselves.

It is to be expected that in a general education so conceived, instrumental and authoritative—not authoritarian—relationships of education will play a greater role than in the other phases of education.

Chapter Seven

Liberal Education

TRADITION DISTINGUISHES liberal education as a career-independent education devoted to the humanities plus some social and natural science and mathematics. That tradition considered from our point of view implies some serious choices in the conduct of education.

According to that view, a liberal education is justified by the self's need to form itself and to determine what it is to want. To be sure, though the subject matters of a general education overlap substantially those of a liberal education, the focus in the latter no longer falls on providing maps. Moreover, the conditions of preparation for effective participation in the society, however much they may affect decisions on the sort of person one is to be, cease to be central. A liberal education that justified itself by the help it offered people for getting on in the world would have confessed itself a fraud. Cynics, looking for just such a justification, consider liberal education a fraud. But if a fraud, it is so for other reasons.

Distinguishing the wants of a human self from distinctively biological drives makes intelligible how a liberal education might provide for the formative function. Drives don't argue; they are what they are, satisfied or not. Wants, on the other hand, in our sense, are educable. Sexual drives are there; one cannot educate a person into or out of them. But whether the individual places sexual drives in the relations of love and friendship depends directly on how the sexual drive is interpreted. One can intervene at that point. Wants like love, friendship, conviviality, prominence, achievement, are no doubt impossible without biological and psychological drives of one sort or another; but wants such as these are intrinsically context bound, not cunning tricks to get around artificial obstacles in order to satisfy drives. The context, of course, is a social one; the self subsists as a self in that context, defines itself there, and forms its interests in a nexus of social relations. More directly than any other form of education, a liberal education presents a new and expanded context for the formation of wants and the reconception of the self. In that context it provides meaning for our actions and criteria for the judgment we render of ourselves.

Montaigne's *Essays* are a superb example of how such meaning and criteria are provided and a self defines itself within the culture of the classic humanities. The innumerable quotations and references in the essays are not excrescences, as they might be for a modern writer whose essential concerns lie elsewhere, but the heart of the matter. They provide the context in terms of which the specific events of Montaigne's life are considered, judged, and summed. The expectations in terms of which he shapes and assesses himself are not inevitable. Others, even among his contemporaries, conceived themselves quite differently, and from the somewhat later Jansenist point of view his conception of what it was to be a human being and what to expect of and for oneself was radically faulty. Not that his kidney stones and his career were altered by the wisdom of the Greek and Latin authors or that he would have constructed the same self without the data of his biology and biography. But how these things were to be taken by him was the palpable force and matter of the inquiry into himself; and to this he brought the full dimensions of his humanism.

His very ruminations on human nature and its limits provide for the point without making it: "Except for you, O man," he writes, fancying the Delphic oracle making the judgment, "each thing studies itself first, and according to its needs, has limits to its labors and desires. There is not a single thing as empty and needy as you, who embrace the universe: you are the investigator without knowledge, the magistrate without jurisdiction, and all in all, the fool of the farce."[1] Animals, as he recognizes, know what they want and seek nothing beyond the satisfaction of their desire. But human beings are not like that. They are "empty and needy." That is how they are human. That is the condition for the truth of the thesis of sociality and the existence of human beings as intrinsically social.

In a general way everyone knows the particular context of a liberal education: the literature, science, art, sociology, psychology, philosophy, history of the civilization, and so on. Nevertheless, changes occur in the fields and in society; there are decisions to be made. Hence the first major problem of a liberal education is to determine what to include in the curriculum. Since our enterprise concerns only the distinctive consequences for the positional interests of students and faculty, I need now only indicate the principles called for in fixing upon the curriculum.

In making the required decisions, an institution appropriately considers both the state of the culture or civilization at the time and, as in general education, the set or classes of persons to whom the liberal education refers. That is the first principle, no less true for being a truism. Science and technology in the eighteenth and nineteenth centuries were often considered outside, or beneath, the scope of a liberal education, and an education considered liberal rather than vocational ministered to classes of persons defined differently than they are now. Greek and Latin in the eighteenth and nineteenth centuries were the mainstays of a liberal education. Now they are an option. Restoring them to their former position would leave the pursuers of a liberal education isolated and restricted in their own world. The civilization has rolled on. On the other hand, the education that shaped its offerings so far as it could to meet the expressed wants and prejudices of its students as it found them would have provided the opportunity for their satisfaction at the cost of surrendering its educative or "liberating" function. That is why religious or military educations, however demanding or praiseworthy they may sometimes be, are not in general "liberal."

In sum, as should surprise no one, to fix upon an adequate curriculum, one neither imposes a pattern upon the students irrelevant to their condition nor attempts to please a market. One tries to come up with a fundamental analysis and judgment of the culture upon which one might obtain a reasoned consensus. Therefore one begins with present practices and their relationships at the institution and argues from there.

The ballet determines the next major principle. The possibilities of reciprocal engagement and happy competition are prime factors in considering which subject matters are to be chosen. For the sake of that possibility a liberal education will naturally tend to provide students with a maximum of appropriate alternatives among which to choose.

The claims of the ballet cannot be ignored without converting what is dealt with from materials for self-construction into information for students' data banks. To suppose that "good teachers" will somehow manage to involve almost anyone in anything they consider worthwhile is a discouraging thought on a par with the dream of a "charismatic" leader who, through the force of personality, leads a people toward ends they might otherwise never embrace. Educational supersalesmen are not to the interest of either student or instructor in the ballet of a liberal education. Students should aspire never to know that "good" a teacher if it is in their interest to determine their own interest. They are nobody's Galateas, no matter how benign and talented the artist.

In consequence of the ballet, the content of the liberal arts and sciences of concern at institutions of higher education becomes responsive to change in students and society—to "fashion." The institution learns how to let go and to open up. In this sense, the life of education becomes, as Justice Holmes said of the law, experience, not logic.

A third principle of selection for liberal education in the arts and sciences can be described as a principle of maximum reach. Programs reach after those parts or aspects of the various disciplines that are as complex, subtle, and demanding as the participants are likely to assimilate at their stage of development. Only this, involving the participants in the processes of a high culture to the degree of their ability, will achieve the development that will satisfy the interests of the participants. As important: in the maximum reach of the education lie the fun, the tension, the excitement that are immediately and most unequivocally to the welfare of the participants in the ballet of education.

It will be observed that what constitutes maximum reach may often come down to a question of what one values. Suppose one says that putting Shakespeare's verse, for example, on the periphery of discussion in order to make Edna St. Vincent Millay's poems central would tend to restrict the reach of the education. Obviously, one says that because one values Shakespeare more highly than Miss Millay, and that opens up a can of worms. The answer is, of course, that despite the extreme character of the example, values are contestable. But from this it does not follow that no contests can be won or lost, only that curricula had better include the study of how contests can be lost or won, in what sense and when.

We are led to the last of our "principles," the one for resolving differences of opinion. Resolution of differences in or about liberal education requires rationality. Few object to this principle in the abstract.

Recently, at major institutions, issue has been angrily joined over what the high culture of the civilization includes. Many have become exercised over the inadequacy of a Eurocentric education and the failure to give the contributions of women and minorities their proper share of attention. The principle of rational resolution requires the agreement of all concerned that so far as possible differences of opinion will be resolved on the merits.

To be sure, people striving strenuously to be rational may be depended upon to disagree often. That, however, no more makes commitment to the principle vacuous than commitment to the relevance of morality renders that commitment vacuous for those lacking a general theory of morality. Even without a clear theory of rationality, one might know enough in a general way to hazard a judgment on the kind of thing the theory might cover; one might fairly make certain assumptions about what would mark a rational process of decision. I hazard a few.

First, the debate will not be "rational" where stands are taken on the basis of political or ethnic loyalties. That changes the game, slides in one debate for another. We thought we were trying to determine what goes into institutions uniquely specialized for intellectual endeavor and progress; it turns out we are talking about who shall overcome. (Perhaps we ought to be talking about that. Perhaps institutions should be transformed into the tools of special interests, provided, naturally, that they are just. That is another issue, a political one.) Next, the reasons that count as good reasons will so count in virtue of a logic discriminable in other domains where good reasons count. If there are good reasons for including the Vedas in higher education, they are good reasons in the sense other reasons are good in determining whether other cultural objects are to be considered in higher education. Lastly, given the appropriateness of the institutional approach, the assumptions of which inform this entire discussion of higher education, due weight and consideration will be given deeply rooted precedent in the evaluation of the practices of higher education. One does not lightly break with such precedent, even if break sometimes one must.

Admittedly, disinterestedness, good reasons, and the seriousness of precedent in higher education are assumptions of a Western civilization now contested. The seriousness of precedent even grants a direct advantage to an education supportive of that civilization. Nevertheless, these assumptions of rationality do not preclude the relevance of the culture of non-Western societies as sources of possible norms for determining what is to be included. They are merely required constraints for the self-reconstruction of the social institutions directly concerned with their culture. Rejecting them as culture-bound dismisses that education the choices of which one presumes to inquire into.

Assuming now what is to be studied provisionally given, how do the participants in the liberal education acquire a "liberal education" in those studies? Just what do they then acquire?

The usual answer is that they acquire understanding of the liberal disciplines and do so by learning what they are taught. That formulation assumes the business of liberal education to consist in the acquisition of knowledge that a discipline or inquiry has certain characteristics and that such and such are the facts it has yielded. Liberal education then becomes the transfer of certain special kinds of information. One learns *about* the science of physics (its "methods," its history, its consequences) and obtains a sampling of what is known about the phenomena of nature. Either the student is supplied with thin generalities about a great many things, including "thinking," "appreciating," "rules" of scientific method, the history of the subject, and so on, plus a certain amount of illustrative material, or the size of the information base upon which the generalizations rest, including the detail required in the analysis of the discipline as such, is increased to approximate the specialist's.

Faculty who conceive their task to be imparting what they know about their disciplines now face a hard choice not only for their discipline but for all the disciplines and parts of disciplines constituting the liberal education taken collectively. Properly suspecting that the generalizing, sampling alternative leaves their learners with little knowledge of substance and/or thin formulae descriptive of procedure in the discipline, they resent being converted into popularizers. Thereupon they seize, ruefully, on the second alternative—to load the undergraduate with as much as the circuits will bear and hope for the best. In the name of the highest standards, they bypass the possibility of a liberal education by definition nonspecialized. Discovering what they already knew—that not many undergraduates can specialize in many fields at once—they risk disdaining their students and their own professed commitment to education as well. In this way educators achieve for their students not only the usual mixture of Gradgrindism, forgetfulness, and weariness with the whole business but an even more basic defeat: in the face of exorbitant demands supposed to determine what it means to know anything, students end up not knowing what it means to know anything. The project of education grinds to a close in a ceremony of pretense, all capped and gowned.

The best practices of faculty and students testify that it need not. While no education occurs without information acquired, the acquisition is a means to a liberal education, not its end. The disjunction of either too much or too little information is, taken in itself, a wrong one.

There is another possibility. Assuming the genuineness of the positional interest in the self and the possibility of a ballet of higher education, the ultimate aim of a liberal education might well be the acquisition of what I shall call "Models." (Hereafter I shall drop the quotes and rely only on the capitalization to differentiate my use from more technical ones.) If that is so, the problem of information then becomes how much and what kind of information best serves their acquisition.

We all have lived with Models all our lives. Models are sets of appropriate expectations for certain kinds of objects of attention. In relation to those expectations people make something or other of some object, or fail to; they feel they have "understood" that object or remain mystified by it. The self itself might be that object. Since people have expectations of themselves and attempt to understand themselves in relation to those expectations, they "know themselves" in virtue of the Models for persons that they acquire.

We read a poem. We do not take the metaphor literally—if we did, we would think it nonsense. Still, there are cues, if we are acquainted with poetry. Sometimes cues fail us. Then we have to make adjustments in our sets of expectations; we have to modify or replace our Models for poetry.

We hear a joke. We understand the thing is a joke though we never heard it before. Nearly anything can be funny, depending on the point of view. We have learned to respond to points of view. We laugh. We have "a sense of humor." The sense of humor is the Model in operation on appropriate cues probably far more complicated than those for recognizing poetry.[2] Still, we have learned to see certain things as humorous or funny. We know what to expect, and how to respond—with a certain kind of seeing.

To perform according to a Model is like speaking another language. Speakers of another language *have* the language. They've got something of the syntax and the vocabulary; they can think in it. To be sure, they do not have all the relevant vocabulary for all interchanges; they are not specialists or professionals. Neither will they grasp everything they hear, any more than the native speaker of a natural language does.[3] Moreover, unlike some professionals, they may not have all that much to say in the language. But though the possessors of a Model in the liberal arts rarely enjoy a facility as great as that of native speakers, you can, as it were, talk to them and explain, within the limits of their intellectual capacity, what they do not understand; you can get to first base with the picture or the poem even if you can't make it home. In sum, having the Model, people can "read" utterances in the domain, and do so without using some other language to make point by point translations according to the rules. Assuming disparities among all or some of the various domains of the liberal arts and sciences, they are, in relation to each of those disparate domains, native speakers. They understand in virtue of what they have become.

Models, which may be conceived as implicit rules or norms for putting things together, face in two directions: toward the objects of attention that, having the characteristics they are perceived to have in virtue of those Models, exhibit or conform to or exemplify them, and toward those who do the work of modeling, those who *have* the Models.

Models as they face their possessors are dispositional states of human beings which cause them to understand some object or set of objects in a particular way. In that sense, people understand in virtue of what they have become and, acquiring a Model, alter themselves. Models, then, are not like cookie cutters pressed into dough. Cookie cutters are tools to be used. Models determine the using of the things at hand. They are equivalent neither to general information about the structure of what they model nor to the maps of a general education, though they presuppose such maps. Rather, they are the norms for dealing with things presupposed by the dealing. As such, they are not "taught" or learned as information is taught or learned. They are not dealt with as maps are when one recognizes or locates a site on a map. If there is a Model for map reading, one doesn't find it on a map. Neither the information acquirers nor the map users change their state or disposition simply by having the information or locating the site. What they know is external to them; the maps are what they have and employ, given certain Models that make the maps meaningful.

At the same time, the employment of the Models—the modeling—does not consist in the deliberate following of a set of detailed instructions. One might, with luck, assemble the parts of a vacuum cleaner that way. But suppose someone asks what to make of a picture or poem. How, the party wants to know, do you go about understanding it? What is one to do? Give directions? People either get the joke or they don't. They have the

Model of a joke sufficiently or they don't. We can't *talk* people without a sense of humor into getting what, if they had one, a few cues would suffice to bring out. Nor can one teach a language by raining down information. Information might serve to break a code, but not to acquire a language. The language cannot be taught without supplying information; hence the need for grammars and dictionaries. But Models are *had*, they are introjected. No matter how many cues are supplied, the one who lacks the Model will not understand.

Finally, because the Models are states or dispositions toward objects, experience in defeating our expectations about those objects can cause us to adjust our Models and learn to make sense of circumstances previously unintelligible. We are then said to have learned from experience something more than facts. Experience can, precisely, change our *minds*. When we conceive of the Models as characteristics of our persons, we conceive of ourselves as performing. The Models become intrinsically performance Models—sets of norms for appropriate action on things of a certain sort and for responses to them. In this sense, the pragmatic motto "Learn by doing!"—which has fallen into such disfavor—is justified. For "doing" means to *use* the Models. To putter about "learning by experience" would be to attempt the performance *without* the Models that make performances— doings—what they are and learning what it is.[4]

One may add that, regardless of how it may be in primary and secondary schools, in a liberal education Models are objectives rather than concessions to psychology made in order to acquire information.

We have been weighing the merits of the Models against the imparting of information for the conduct of liberal education. But there is, among the Models themselves, a relationship that deserves comment: where the Models for appreciation and those for action and knowledge are to be applied has become confused.

It is the confusion, not the relative positions in the curriculum of the arts as compared with the physical and social sciences, that concerns us.

First, it must be emphasized that the Models of perception and discrimination in the arts and, indeed, in human affairs generally, are still performance Models, worked out in appropriate enterprises of the ballet. To say that does not confuse them with the Models for science or practical affairs. Even connoisseurship is acquired in terms of the critical interchange among the participants before the objects of its concern; Models of value and discrimination are at least as necessary there as for the appreciation of jokes. (We shall later on see how the appreciation and appraising of the arts is linked to the doing of the arts, rather in the way that no one who could not make a joke is likely to get one.) Similarly, scholarship, though often identified with what scholars have lodged in their memory, can be conceived as a way, established in accordance with some Model, of acquiring information and dealing with it. This much said, however, it does not follow that, having cheerfully admitted the relevance of performance Models to liberal education, one appropriately takes the Models for what amounts to aesthetic performance for the primary Model of liberal education.

Now I do not think that is an idle observation. In order to establish a distinctive character for such education, it is tempting to deal with science, politics, ethics—the whole gambit of concerns—primarily as possible objects of aesthetic attention rather than as activities with their own distinctive values. There is no denying that such a move is possible. One could become a connoisseur of politics, an entranced witness of the practices and malpractices of ethics. All human affairs are subject to such a grasp; the entire ballet could now be made to center about the worst and the best of them, distinguishing, criticizing, perceiving, assessing. We are become as gods. But we are not gods; we end deprived as human beings. Having suffered the consequences of confusing the practices of liberal education of the

Models for the sciences, politics, and ethics with the Models of aesthetics, the participants in that education no longer grasp what it is to know or act. They end with pictures in the head.

A serious difficulty—that of distinguishing the norms of the practice in art, science, philosophy, religion, scholarship, and so on—now arises for those who would employ the Models, regardless of how they would do so. The Models are not given; they must be discriminated in the practices of those domains. What, actually, are they? To answer that question represents a primary responsibility of any education genuinely concerned with performance. Carrying further the language analogy: one can, and does, ask even of native speakers whether they speak well. The language was there before the speaker. The discipline was there before the inquirer. In what shall the person become practiced?

The problem is familiar to those interested in the foundations of disciplines. Saying what the Models are goes to those foundations. On the one hand, a response depends upon the norms that scientists, artists, mathematicians, poets do in fact follow. On the other, they may get these norms wrong or poorly in their practice. Scientists, artists, and the rest commonly differ among themselves in their very address to some matters they would take to be essential to any education. They are often quick to insist that their colleagues err or are otherwise inadequate in their very concept of their inquiry. Any resolution of their disagreements may involve a reformulation of the field itself. Compounding the difficulty further still, in the pursuit of actual problems the boundaries among the disciplines and parts of disciplines to which the Models pertain constantly shift, with the result that the very process of specifying a living Model entails a position on the Model. Description and prescription have become inseparable, to the complication of both.

Some important morals follow for the attainment of Models in liberal education. The first, taken seriously at some institutions though hardly all, is that those who lead the dance in which the Models are formed must themselves be active in the current work of their fields. Another is that since the boundaries of those "fields" are, at their cutting edge, often problematic, those who seek Models—students and faculty alike—commit themselves to an active and curious examination of inquiries contiguous to their own. The third, as suggested earlier, is that simply to ask which are the Models to be "taught," to be laid down and imparted like the fingering of the seventh position on the violin, ends rather than grounds the activity of liberal education pertinent to a changing culture.

A most important fourth follows: that the participants in a liberal education accept the fact that in the processes of a liberal education we do not always know or agree upon what it means to know, make, or do and that we may move from point to point divided in our own minds. This will seem like a confession of the folly of Models. But it need not, any more than confusion and disagreement among those who work in a discipline constitute a confession of the folly of the discipline modeled. Provided the center of the discipline holds, this indeterminacy of Models, rather than obstructing the movement of the liberal ballet, will provide it with a further dimension. The indeterminacy of Models in education comes to constitute a part of the process through which students and faculty function as principal participants quite as a parallel indeterminacy comes to constitute a part of the process through which people function most profoundly in their fields.

In sum, the differences among proposals for the Models do not make the Models useless. On the contrary, the very differences—when the attempt is made to resolve them—give to the Models a large part of their function in forming minds. The difficulty with Models is a virtue.

Liberal education as here described meets the positional interests of students and faculty in virtue of those Models. For, to begin with, performance Models are not only Models *for* understanding the how and why of presented materials. In themselves, in virtue of their generality and often their indeterminacy, they face forward toward the future. Those who have them know how to make sense of what they know only incompletely and how to be puzzled when they ought. The Models are therefore the fundamental means for entering as a modest participant the active life of the culture and civilization. In a degree, partially (how many Models can any individual assimilate?), those who possess them are at home.

Next, Models enable participants in the educative process to say what they want—not in detail, to be sure, but sufficiently to help them determine what to include or exclude. In transforming individuals into performers of a certain sort—not just rule followers—in the various areas in which they may indeed enter, the Models form sensitivities: not only for eighteenth-century music, but also for attentiveness of a certain sort; not only for ancient Greek, but also for subtlety and the possibilities of languages in use; not for the study of Plato alone, which then would be reduced to reportage without the interest in whether the argument held water, but also in the weight of argument; not just for *King Lear*, but for the doom of human life that is its theme. Through Models the self's opening on its world is extended. Models are not the pedagogic means to a liberal education but its end.

Lastly and most fundamentally, there is the self-formative consequence of a liberal education shaped in the Models illustrated early in the chapter by the case of Montaigne. Those who have assimilated them conceive themselves differently, which does not render the selfish unselfish or the unselfish selfish. The meaning of selfishness or unselfishness for the individual changes as the dispositions these terms may designate occur in new relationships and in relation to altered beliefs. So in one sense the old self continues; the needs, the drives, the hang-ups persist. But now they have come to mean something entirely new to the self that suffers them. The self has grasped itself as a kind of token in another, if related, grammar. Having significance for itself in context, it construes its interests in a certain way and hence re-forms itself. It lays itself off on new coordinates.

In making choices, then, one formed in the Models makes a fool of oneself, if one does, in different ways, in the light of different alternatives. Except for the Models, certain possibilities would never have come into being and certain others would have been refined out of recognition. One sees the world differently. The world changes not only with respect to judgments of the better and the worse in a discipline but also with respect to the reaches of possibility outside the specific discipline. For there is no way of confining in advance the attitudes, sensitivities, expectations one has acquired in the effort to understand this science or that art to this science or that art—not where the "learning" of it is, in virtue of a Model, a function of the self itself and not a form of training.

A more familiar way of justifying the choice of a liberal education as an education in Models would be to say that a liberal education forms a "Mind." Provided, as has been proposed, that to have a "mind" means to have, in virtue of a wide-ranging and profound education, a distinctive mode of address to problems that cannot be handled as problems in rule following and not an unusually large accumulation of knowledge *that*, my claim comes to this: that Mind, conceived through the assimilation of Models in a ballet of liberal education, is in the fundamental and essential interest of the human self or "psyche" that can manage it.

Why should anyone labor to have a Mind in this sense to the degree that he or she can? The answer that mind or intellect is to the self-interest of those who can manage it is not as self-evident as educators like to assume when they defend the value of a liberal education. Intellect is not the only "fundamental and essential" interest. "Mind," as interpreted here, has a hard time in the world precisely because it entails the assimilation of the Models into the self. If all that Mind and a liberal education entailed were more or less recondite information about the classics, philosophy, and the rest of the curriculum, at worst they would be irrelevant to the prospects of the individual; liberal education might be a waste of time, perhaps, but it would do little harm. Taken seriously, however, liberal education entails opening the self, *through* its accomplishments, to frustration and boredom when the person lives effectively in the world and to ineffectiveness and the attendant disasters when he or she seeks to live well.

The Pollyannas of liberal education blithely ignore the way the world goes. All but the luckiest of those in liberal education are impaled more or less painfully upon the choice of making out or going for what they want. The clear, flat choice of the education that offers the Mind of the Models implies what we probably will never have: the Good Society that has banished incoherence. Caught in their own publicity, the Pollyannas have forgotten the interest in coherence and the obstacles in the way of attaining it.[5]

Still, those who have the necessary kinds of character and intelligence for grasping and employing the Models of a liberal education might have this to say in defense of their doing so: first, in the manner of John Stuart Mill, that those who have experienced those Models would have no doubt of their choice were the choice presented to them; second, that, pressed for their choice, those same persons would see the question as a question of a choice of themselves, of their existence versus their nonexistence; third, that they would defend the virtue of their minded existence, if they thought it needed defense, on the one hand by the sense of heightened being it gives them, and, on the other, by its value in formulating and resolving the problems they face. Those who place their bets on mind might conceive that they just might win their wager against disjointedness in their lives or, losing it, provided they are lucky, gain a shot at creativity.

Chapter Eight

Literature, Science, Philosophy

LET US NOW TRY MORE specifically to illustrate what the use of Models might imply for liberal education in three of its established domains: literature, physics, and philosophy. How indispensable mathematics, the social sciences, psychology, language, and linguistics are and to what extent each is important I do not attempt to say. Since students' necessary freedom to choose their studies requires a wide range of alternatives, there is no need here to work up a principle for granting some subjects in the tradition priority over others.

The study of literature seems inseparable from a liberal education. In recent times, however, some scholars have taken literature as a kind of science. The scientific study of literature is, in the abstract, as plausible as the scientific study of anything else; one might inquire into the psychology of literary production and appreciation, their relation to social conditions, semiotics, hermeneutics, and a raft of matters from the logic of literature's metaphor and syntax to its truth claims. But these studies, despite their real merits, do not offer the possibilities for a liberal education to be found in the study of literature in the more traditional sense of an examination and assessment of particular works in regard to their nature, genuineness, functioning, and literary merit. Few, one trusts, will question the importance of such possibilities to a liberal education, however much they prefer to direct their scholarly inquiries in other directions.

"Literature" in our traditional sense, it will be immediately noted, comprises many distinct genres. That would seem to raise an objection to the attempt to work out in the educational ballet a single Model for literature. On the other hand, there is no logical argument against a plurality of related Models in a domain. In literature, a plurality of Models contributes to the subject's utility for the purposes of higher education. While drama, fiction, essay, poetry are all of them to be differentiated, each generates different sets of expectations with respect to different cues and different implicit rules for appropriate responses. Yet rarely are those different Models so different that they in no way bear on one another. One insists upon not confusing poetry and essays or fiction and theater, upon keeping one's categories clean. Still, there is—or was—blank verse in theater, fiction in poetry, essay in drama, and so on. The Models separate and meld, generating new forms and making old ones irrelevant to the development of the arts. So, because their use involves defining the literary domain and its possibilities, the attempt to discern them entails their construction and reconstruction; their use in the critical appreciation of "literature" entails involvement in the creative labors of the domain. In effect, the positional interest in determining what one is to like or want is met not by the application of a series of given, approved tastes but by an active process of participation in which individuals form judgments and preferences.

The enemy of literature in the projects of liberal education, as in literature itself, is not the shifting diversity of its Models. It is the classical. By that I do not at all mean the particular works designated as classics. These are part and parcel of literature's life. The enemy is the status of the objects as classic—as standard, indisputable, exclusive arbiters of taste. That status is as inimical to education as it is to a nonrepetitious literature. For participants in the ballet are skeptical, challenging; they proffer their own reasons, demand to be convinced by those of others. They challenge one another's preferences and, in being challenged, are induced to challenge themselves. They are, therefore, on the make. They seek the better, stronger judgment, the more profound understanding. "Taste" becomes the outcome of the forming of the Models in the ballet, not the premise.

Taste is usually considered a matter of taste. De gustibus . . . But if there is no argument about tastes, then if anything is to be better than anything else, the only alternative is to follow the rules, follow the classics, don't argue. Classicism and relativism both terminate the ballet; the end is either the consumerism of the elegant or the consumerism of Everyman. So in order to clarify the relevance to liberal education of exploring the Models of literature, let us say that one seeks through those Models not expressions of "refined and superior taste" but "artistically relevant judgments." The expression, though clumsy, may help skirt committing education in literature and art in general to either the snobberies of higher education or the collapse of judgment.

In the pursuit of literature and its parts, liberal education, on the approach proposed here, would find the focus of its enterprise in those judgments that made a difference for the doing of literature, hence "artistically relevant," rather than in those that expressed substantially approved tastes. The future is the name of that game, and that future includes the redoing of the past as much as the establishment of limits and possibilities for the as yet unwritten. The participants of liberal education enter the ballet to the degree in which they see themselves in a literary enterprise. Those proposing judgments of the relevant and the irrelevant, of the better and the worse, would be proposing them from the point of view of members of the enterprise even if no one outside the classroom paid them any attention. They would have considered their judgments as implying precedents for dealing with literary objects in ways not all that different from the

way judges in superior courts of law might propose judgments—
not as fiats of taste, but rather in the light of the precedents, of
the instant case and of their concern for the consequences.[1]

Suppose, then, that in appropriately reasoned differences of
opinion judgments of literature constituted, or presupposed,
judgments on the appropriate future for that literature. Would
not a liberal education caught up in the generation of Models
prefer to work on such an assumption? There are live issues,
even if ultimately sheer unquestioned and unalterable prejudices
make their appearance. Ultimately is later on. In the meanwhile, argument proceeds, bases are sought for agreement, ex-
periment is possible, Models are made and remade in which
judgments would be guided and examined. One seeks to understand what the poet accomplished and the relationship of the ac-
complishment to the relevant environment. One seeks to know
as intimately as possible the plays or poems "in themselves" and
in the relationships that make it possible to distinguish how
they are what they are and not something else. The end, if the
object is a liberal education, becomes not erudition as such but
the development of Models in order to distinguish choices the
poet might have made, to compare them with those actually
made by this poet or other poets under relevant circumstances,
to distinguish the relevant circumstances from the irrelevant,
to ask what shape of poetry would justify the judgment, what
would not.

Significant consequences then follow for the self-interested.
Their enterprises now generate not only a series of recommen-
dations for the preferred performance of poetry but the occasion
and provocation of style or address in the dance of education.
Members of the ballet are no mere technicians coolly appraising
an object in their field and arguing with their colleagues, even if
technical inquiry increases the opportunity to expand involvements and sensitivities. Members of the ballet, if not become
poets, have at least found the sense and feel of poetry that may
remain after the recollection of the parts and structure of the

material studied has gone. They have become imprinted. Where a Model's imprintment is the end there is less need to worry over what serves as the best possible sample of the enterprise for the student and the instructor, and more about what will best suit their character and purposes. Attempts to determine the Great Books that everyone, irrespective of individual requirements, should have read are as beside the point as analogous attempts to list the information everyone should have after passing through the educational maze.

The clearest and most obvious effect of the domain of literature upon the participants, however, consists in this: the literary arts are preeminently modes of socialization. In those arts, students encounter the thoughts, feelings, experiences of what used to be called significant others. Whether or not those others happen to exist is unimportant. Given that selves define themselves in relation to others, Models for being human are refined and adjusted. Expectations and perceptions alter. The cast of characters, the repertoire of stories and of speeches encountered in the literary pursuit may dim over time; but the altered Models for apprehending other human beings may persist indefinitely. We have done better than file away cultural artifacts. We have assimilated shared contexts for the grasp of human experience.

Instruction in the sciences exhibits more clearly still the performative aspect of Models in the liberal education. People in the sciences are less concerned than those in the humanities with building Memorials to past greatness and more skeptical of leaving a deposit of what everyone ought to know. The sciences are present- and action-oriented. People do science; one does not "know" science unless in some measure one would know how to go about doing it. Few, except for philosophers and historians of science and culture, now need to read Newton as writers, critics, and dramatists need to read Shakespeare.

The reason to doubt that the accumulation of scientific facts constitutes the end of scientific education requires no special insight. Attempting to distinguish in the overwhelming mass of scientific knowledge what everybody ought to know seems hopeless. Especially those who have devoted their lives to the sciences will feel at a loss if they are supposed to do in the sciences what instructors are often supposed to do in the humanities, which is to present the core of the culture. Having accepted that objective for the humanities, naturally they think the humanities soft and the sciences hard; for they do not conceive themselves intellectually inferior to their colleagues in the humanities, let alone to their colleagues' students.

As a matter of course, people in the sciences take their primary contribution to the liberal education to be to communicate some grasp of the methods and approaches of the various sciences to all their students while providing a preprofessional training for those who go on. Studies are conducted through close reading, problems, and experiments. The reading is conducted for the sake of the problems; experiments make sense of the reading. In the physical sciences, learning involves doing the kind of thing done in the sciences. Though the problems and experiments may be pro forma, they press students to become, in a modest way, physicists or chemists. Of relevance here, however, is not how the appropriate Models are formed but how their assimilation relates to self-interest.

How, then, do the sciences contribute to self-formation? First and foremost from the point of view of a liberal education, they offer Models for how to be in the world. Science is often praised for its consequences. Less frequently acknowledged is that it requires persons of a certain sort to produce those consequences. If this constructive demand seems strange, it is only because of the widespread habit of separating off the self's identity from what the self does, of presupposing a completely formed self deciding what to do with itself, as when one asks what shall *I* do with *myself.* The parallel lies less with Ryle's ghost in the machine, which raises ontological questions, than with the driver of a car and the car, which raises practical ones. Where does the driver want to go with the car? There is the driver, who chooses his destination for his own reasons, and there is the car, from which he walks away pretty much as he was when he got in.

Neither the culture nor the individual walks away unchanged from the practice of the sciences.[2] The actuality of science historically engenders the possibility of the new man or woman. To be sure, all human conditions place a premium upon the use of intelligence and attentiveness to the environment. Even so, "scientific" attitudes, perspectives, and attentiveness do not under all circumstances tend to become dominant; magic and submission may. For science to dominate, the community must be organized around appropriate ways of standing in relation to beliefs—must engender the habit, the internal need to subject beliefs to criticism, refinement, persistent adjustment and re-adjustment. Persons so ingrained may simultaneously maintain quite different attitudes; rationality can coexist with very strange bedfellows. A Newton can take numerology seriously. Yet insofar as persons are rational, they inhabit a new community, a community that changes them. Self-criticism becomes possible, not just as a bite of social conscience, but as the factual, objective assessment of where they stand. It becomes possible to speak of an ideal of the truth that means more than the certainty of one's initial prejudice. A kind of practical humility has been born.

None of this implies that assimilating the Model of a science (inevitably a performance Model) always carries over to every domain in which it might apply. Still, a possibility has been presented live to the individual. When that happens, the first step has been taken, followed up or not, toward a commitment to a more extensive engagement in an altered life. While the liberal education through its Models of the sciences, or indeed of any of its disciplines, can hardly save the world or the soul, it can offer its beneficiaries a possibility for shaping themselves that must be advantageous to those prepared to acknowledge incompleteness.

For those who go on to do the sciences more or less professionally, the different styles and elegances made available by the different sciences through their different procedures will matter essentially. For the others, however, and for the purposes of the liberal education, the question of plural Models is of lesser moment. How the Models of the sciences differ matters less than the common rationality they employ. The examples differ; the moral remains in most respects the same.

Another moral exists for the formation of the self through the Models of the sciences related to but not quite identical with that of a shared commitment to rationality: through the sciences and their Models scientific prediction and control become systematized and real. I am making a statement not about the pragmatic interpretation of science but about people. A self becomes a predicting, controlling self, a knowledge user in the attainment of its ends, not simply a power user; and this creates a unique sense of self and of what it wants. Technology, in a word, has appeared and shapes human development. Fears and hopes quite outside the formal sciences change in the light of possible realization and substitute contingencies for dreams. Specific information makes certain ends preposterous and pulls others suddenly within grasp. The expectations grounding choices are assessed for their probabilities. Control over events, even if things do not quite work out, has become a permanent, pressing possibility one can no longer ignore and has given birth to a new anxiety—that one might fail where one might have succeeded. One lives, in however confined a space, in the awareness of new worlds just over the lip of the horizon, and in the expectation that these worlds might be dealt with. The Model of the sciences, in its most general form, in the process of offering a generalized effectiveness in the world, has altered the self and its expectations, and in doing so justified the presence of science in a liberal education.

The Models of the sciences bear on self-interest in still another way, one which receives little notice when, as under present social conditions, technology and the economy preempt attention. Involvement in the ballets that feature the sciences may foster a particular manner of existing for those capable of it, an impersonal mode that demands not self-subordination but self-forgetfulness in an intrigued concentration on the world. The sciences and math are not alone in offering that possibility. The fine arts themselves, at their height, are not mere exercises in self-expression, even though there, as elsewhere, the self is in some sense expressed; they, too, may entail a pouring out upon a subject matter. My point is merely that grasping the natural sciences in the light of the Models leaves no room for self-concern or self-exploitation or ulterior motive. In consequence, some find in the sciences a kind of peace. That is one reward of the free, the liberal (or liberated) mind, and very much to the welfare of the individual.[3]

Science-tasting and roaming among the visions of Very Great Scientists—in a word, becoming cultured in science—is not the point now, whatever may be said in its favor. The grappling with the material—the doing of the inquiry and not just the observing of the results, however interesting—realizes the self's interest in an outward turning. That is one reason the Models of performance become so central in the liberal education.

Consider now philosophy. Philosophy has a distinctive place in the program of a liberal education that humanists and classical scholars on one hand and people in the sciences on the other frequently misunderstand. Humanists would like to see philosophy done in the spirit of those who acquire and explore the benefactions of a spiritual inheritance. People in the sciences, insofar as they take the subject seriously rather than as another case of dedication to worthy old Monuments ("Culture"), would find it natural to regard it as a kind of science or adjunct to science. Philosophers themselves often split along these as along most other lines.

Both sides miss the nature of the Models philosophy might

offer liberal education. They do not necessarily miss them because of mistaken notions of the proper problems of philosophy; what philosophy deals with represents a philosophical problem itself, and the pursuit of that problem an exercise in intellectual self-awareness of the sort that one might expect of the liberally educated individual. But rather than venturing to draw the line around where one properly enters and leaves philosophy, let us for the purposes of the liberal education take its problems as we find them in the history of the subject and require of them only that as themes of the liberal education they be open to reasoned argument. Then we discover that confusion over the Models philosophy offers the liberally educated tends to arise at least in part because one finds in the problems of the subject fundamental similarities to both the sciences and the so-called humanities.

Humanists approaching philosophy typically imagine that the Models enable or should enable us to grasp the import of certain great moments or Traditions in their relation to history. To understand philosophy is, for them, preeminently to understand the history of the human mind or, if the end is not historical, to grasp it as a work of art. The perspective need not be uncritical or obscurantist. But whether it is or not, "scientific" or technical philosophy receives scant appreciation. Those, on the other hand, who deal with philosophy from a technical point of view see it, like the sciences, concerned—though for the most part without the experimental methods—with the progress of inquiry into specific, evolving problems.

There is no question that philosophical activity is often carried on in that way, especially when critical materials from mathematics, science, and computer science enter the picture. (Not long ago, the break between the two ways of conceiving the subject contributed to a split in the organization of the philosophical "profession.") But I am not about to advocate either traditionally oriented or, to use the current label, "analytic" philosophy—although a non-analytic philosophy would seem to have lost its claim to be philosophy in any sense—for the purposes of constituting Models in liberal education. I do not wish to say even that the discipline is valuable because one can find both analytic and more traditional performances in it. My point is that the peculiar, although not the sole, value of the discipline for liberal education consists in the possibility of performing philosophy both ways as a single project. Such a performance may achieve what the other humanities and the sciences cannot: a Model for the engagement of the past with the present in an ongoing movement to achieve the best grounded view attainable.

In philosophy at least, the debate with those parts of the past relevant to the state of the argument never ceases; nobody is debarred for being dead. One argues with one's Socrates. He is not simply a testimonial to the human spirit. We take him seriously, as antagonist or ally or both. Therefore, he must be interpreted, like the people we know personally, in his context before we can know what he is saying. Even so, we are not interested in seeing what our Socrates has to say just to grasp and appreciate his intent. We insist on assessing the strength of that intent. We did not debate with King Lear. Hence philosophy's divergence from the other humanities. At the same time, the very absence of substantial progress in the reasoned resolution of some philosophical problems provides the occasion for Models that engage the past in a way made pointless for the sciences by the rapidity and continuity of their advance.

What, then, is the use of these Models in an engagement that leaves little or nothing settled? It is not to satisfy an insatiable demand for clarity for the sake of clarity—the telephone book makes many clear statements—but to clarify matters close to the heart of human life and knowledge. Given the understanding that human life and knowledge, both, go on, we cannot aim to know only what we know already, although we would find ourselves in a distressing mess if we did not also aim at that. Perhaps fending off the possibility of an uncertainty built into the nature of our condition lies at the edge of peoples' minds when they confine philosophy, taken as the pursuit of things that matter most, to eternal problems and eternal truth. In that event, sheer self-interest tells them to come off it. We change, society changes, knowledge explodes; and while we may, from time to time, prove adequate to our occasions, that we know what we want is a gamble we often lose. Hoping to save our skins, we are compelled to press on to new confusions. Philosophy confronts a perpetual need to reconfront ourselves, our beliefs, and our values in relation to what we are, have been, and might be.

One particular reason enables those who have the Model to face time and change. Not only does philosophical inquiry press for clarity under changing circumstances; it does so by the direct consideration of its own activities and those of the other disciplines. So people speak of the philosophy of science, law, literature, and so on, but do not necessarily expect new disclosures of the kind a scientist, lawyer, or writer would contribute. Philosophers engage one another over the nature and validity of the Models established. For the liberally educated, therefore, philosophy furnishes not a royal road to knowledge but a further way of perceiving the drift of an inquiry and of distinguishing what it is from what it is not, however provisionally and skeptically. Philosophy is the direct reflex to transition in the Models and, as such, not confined to professional philosophers; and that is one reason for its utility for people to whom the Models of their education are a positional interest.

We may go one step further in reaching for the point of philosophy in self-formation. Philosophical inquiry seeks not only to understand the Models of the other disciplines; it seeks to relate them. I do not of course mean that it invariably succeeds or that if it succeeds it is likely to do so for very long as the disciplines develop. Still, historically and inevitably, philosophers have considered the bearings of the Models on one another as they sought to determine what the Models were and how they might be justified. Science, history, literature, art, mathematics, psychology—their relations generate the problems of their definition.[4] Together, their Models create a problem of Mind other than the ontological problem of consciousness or of the working of the mind—the substantive problem of what it means to know and to act in all the complexities of knowing and acting in specific situations. People have lived without reference to that problem. Still, however implicitly, they respond to it and, to the extent they do, define themselves and their wants in the widest context of the civilization.

To sum, then, the proposed view of liberal education: in relation to the positional interest in self, a liberal education entails the assimilation of Models. In philosophy, science, literature—in all the domains of liberal education—there are Models for performance. That is, these domains entail, to use an old distinction, both knowledge *that* such and such is the case and knowledge *how* ("know-how") to do certain sorts of things, which is not equivalent to the knowledge *that* one might have of knowledge *how*. Knowledge *how* most assuredly requires knowledge *that* what is the case is indeed the case, but makes use of the data provided for purposes and in contexts that make the relationship of information to action very different from logical application.

It follows that if philosophy, science, or literature and other disciplines are addressed from the participants' point of view and their end is seen as proffering only or primarily knowledge *that* the disciplines tell us such and such or, for that matter, that the disciplines have in fact certain characteristics and certain theories, they have been much misunderstood. An education proceeding on that assumption would have set its hopes on the termination of liberal education. In place of the gamble of higher education, it would have chosen certainty, and in place of the Models of performance, contemplation.

These Models, it must be remembered, derive from a consideration of liberal education in its present state. In concentrating on liberal education as it is, I have paid insufficient attention to what it might become. Models outside the province of the established disciplines might be found feasible and desirable for the participants and society as a whole. The environing society may reach into the inner core of liberal education and generate enterprises outside the normal scope of the arts and sciences. In problems may begin opportunities for the fashioning of new Models for liberal education.

Newspapers report horror stories of the relations among white males, blacks, chicanos, and women on the campuses of the country. My example concerns merely the breakdown of civility, not discriminations, violence, or struggles for power. On a California campus not long ago, two more or less drunk fraternity men accosted two black women and made advances to them that mocked and derogated them as women and as blacks. Something, it was agreed, ought to be done. But what? If every time men and women propositioned one another it constituted an offense there would be no end of offenses. Was nothing therefore to be done about it—suspension, dismissal? Taking action seemed to require penalizing the offenders for their egregious behavior by whatever means their institution had available. If an appropriate penalty could be devised, a penalty seemed indeed called for.

Penalties, however, miss the essential point for an institution of higher education. They tend to disguise the need for a decision on the province of higher education—whether it shall or shall not cover the coming to be of persons in the relationships of civilization. Not only had the women been assaulted, verbally if not physically; the action of liberal education had, to the extent the malefactors had been exposed to it, failed, and the nature of the failure had been spread before the community in the character of the assault.

For the particular males involved, of course, no education might have had any prospect of success. Yet their behavior raises an implicit question. Might the process of education have been organized not indeed to punish or even to rehabilitate the offenders but specifically to foster the development of persons for whom such miserable behavior would constitute an affront to themselves as well as to the women? Investigations into styles and modes of life for human beings in relation to one another and of their consequences are undertaken in an ad hoc fashion at most colleges and universities; but the resources of the social sciences, history, anthropology, philosophy might conceivably be marshalled to create alternate Models for the daily performance of students who have not fixed their wants or themselves in concrete and for whom self-formation is a real possibility. I refer not to "interdisciplinary studies," combinations of this and that, but to reorganizations and reinterpretations of resources at hand for the sake of clearer, sharper Models of possible human relations.

Obviously, I have no specific curriculum to propose. But the conceiving of new or alternate modes of address to other human beings is not primarily a question of accumulating certain kinds of information to be organized in a curriculum. It is instead a question of an awareness of the possibilities of the different kinds of expectations and the cues and responses that persons develop, the internalization of a sensibility to the passing relations of life. In a word, it is a question of the Models of civility.

If there is a "method" of science, perhaps there might be a method or methods of civility. We need make no propaganda. We do not insist on one code for the relationships of civility any more than we insist on one universal language; the syntax and the vocabulary are always in some measure arbitrary. Still, what is conveyed is not therefore arbitrary. The civility or insult lies in the import. We leave the final consequences of the perception of the Models of civility, as perforce we must, to the individual, and do so on the wager that the more "minded" relations become the less likely the degradation of the casual assault.

All this, of course, is at once sketchy and highly speculative. It may nevertheless indicate a further direction for the development of the Models of civilization beyond the arts and sciences.

Chapter Nine

Higher Education and the Professions

THE COMMENTS THAT FOLLOW are, for the most part, addressed not to the requirements of the particular kinds of professional schools but to the policy choices required of any of them, as professional schools, at the university.

Historically, professions like law and medicine were first entered largely through apprenticeship. Only in the nineteenth century did formal schools enter the picture to any considerable extent, and not till the latter part of the century were these schools raised to university grade.[1] In consequence, education for the professions initially emphasized treating them as vocations like any others. That meant, of course, treating them entirely in their relationships to what I have called the interest in effectiveness. Why, then, has that education become an essential part of today's university, and what does this transition imply for the choices of a professional education considered properly a part of higher education at the university?

In substantial measure, the waning importance of formal apprenticeship and the rise of professional education at universities surely reflect a continuously complicating technology and the requirements for professional activity in a complicating society. Knowledge, increasing and deepening at a rate that differentiates the present from other times, renders the apprenticeship system obsolete. Physicians need a battery of experts to prepare them not only in medicine proper but in the chemistry, physiology, physics, biomedical engineering, and so on presupposed by contemporary medical practice. The law, with the enormous expansion of business and production, the advent of new forms of property and finance, the appearance of societies in which business, production, property, and finance must be governed and regulated, engenders parallel consequences. Apprenticeship cannot occupy the center even if in an obvious sense every new graduate of law school, medical school, or, for that matter, business school, serves an indispensable de facto apprenticeship.[2]

The natural home of the professions, therefore, becomes the university, where the specific involvement with the cognitive conditions of contemporary civilization is to be found. The status of a practice as a profession is defined less by the work it accomplishes in society at large than by access to and utilization of the resources of society's knowledge centers. The status of a vocation shifts with the degree to which the apparatus of higher education pertains. The list of professions lengthens and a major gap develops, with extraordinary consequences for the lives of those involved, between the vocations that are unqualifiedly professions and those that are not.

Still, professional educations preserve themselves as such on another dimension than the relationship to the higher education of which they are a part: they have, patently, engaged themselves to the achievement of specific jobs in society; their pursuit faces outward in ways in which the pursuit of the liberal arts and sciences does not. For this reason professional educations mark the most direct approach taken by higher education toward the coherence of the interests in self and the demands for effectiveness. The profession serves two masters: the discipline of the profession, which the professional schools are expected to construct, and the public.

Such, roughly, is the institutional context in which, as I take it here, professional schools may justify their major policy choices. They have not abandoned thereby the self-interest of their students or even modified their commitment to it; for the students have chosen, as the expression goes, what they want to be—doctors, lawyers, teachers, business *machers*, engineers. At the same time, the students have a very imperfect idea of how to be what they want to be, which is why they attend the school. The institution offers them a Model or Models for being a professional—for becoming what they intend. (The state of becoming a lawyer is far from the same as the state of being a lawyer.) In this way the interest in self is served along with and in virtue of the interest in effectiveness. It seems appropriate to call the Models sought for "coherence Models." Those who set the policies of the school can only hope, and do their best to ensure, that those Models attained and defining the individual will not in the end turn disastrous to one who lives in many other contexts beside the professional.

What sorts of Models will the professional schools at the university seek to construct when they consider themselves part of higher education and recognize the service they perform?

Most generally, the Models constructed will depend upon the social interchanges I have called the ballet of higher education. Though in some ways similar, they differ from those of undergraduate education in theme, styles, and the persons with whom the students have to deal. Those with whom students engage may have more prescribed and varied parts to play than instructor and student. Also, those to whom students are expected to minister—client, patient, and so on—may become part of the ballet in the practicum or its equivalent. So every school that hopes to construct professional Models will have considered very carefully the special network of relationships among the proper participants in the dance.

The first and most obvious choice of Models for professional schools concerns the professional as the expert. The question for the schools is what it means to be an expert. On one view, experts are those with the complex information of the schools at their disposal; students then pass or fail depending on whether they have met the standards, since their business after graduation is to apply that information. Librarians, on some conceptions of what it means to be a librarian, may see their business that way.

Not all professional schools by any means welcome that Model of professionalism as expertise. Professional schools, partly in consequence of the flood of information that no one can manage anyway—and more perhaps in consequence of the practical need to apply judgment with what information seems available—typically reject it. Aware that even the best will be unable to satisfy the demands of the knowledge imperative and, what is more, may not want to, they will aim at Models that approximate those of a liberal education and seek to prepare their students to distinguish the relevant from the irrelevant and knowledge from ignorance. They are the heirs and preservers of perspective of liberal attitudes in the performance of specific functions in society.

A more controverted choice of Models results directly from the tension between the ministry of the professional school to the needs of the public and the conditions of its existence as a species of graduate education. Law students pressing for acquisition of the skills and experience directly and immediately valuable for working in the legal system furnish a good example. They see the point of learning how the courthouse works. They miss the point of the concern that professors often have for the theory of the law and for the scholarship that wins no cases and find achievement in these matters of little or no relevance to selecting a faculty. On both sides of the argument the issue may then seem like the ancient one between theory and practice. But in fact students who sharply distinguish theory and practice have no objection whatsoever to elaborate theories of society and social welfare, while their opponents hardly deny that lawyers must be given something of the wherewithal to practice.

The law school, or, with greater or lesser urgency, any other professional school, faces these alternatives: to educate graduates according to the Model of either the faculty or the practitioner, to educate some according to one Model and others according to the other, or to take steps toward a Model that faces both ways, namely, a coherence Model.

The first function of such a Model would be to apprehend the present conditions and methods of practice in the context that shows them as possibilities rather than as inevitable constraints on practice. The practice itself is conceived in relation not just to the future of the practitioner but to its own future and past. Persons practicing in the law, or business, or medicine, or engineering, or teaching, when they know what they are doing, know not only that they are taking a particular action, they know what that action means in the context of the present state of the profession and for its possible future.

Of course, those who work in a profession don't have to know such things. To practice, they need only know what is required to make the system work for their own purposes. A coherence Model for professional schools, however, projects more than a way of knowing the job to be done and more than a context for making sense of it; it projects a complex of obligations, rights, privileges, and preferences, all of which must be dealt with if the individual is to be a professional. The Model prepares for the occupation of a social position that will bear on the individual's decisions. Not only is work done; a relationship with the others through whom that work is done must be maintained. Since that complex relationship is at critical points problematic in the changing environment for which the professional is being prepared, it may require the most careful consideration of the schools as they go about presenting their Model of a professional. They must be prepared to deal with the complex of obligations, rights, privileges, and preferences that the graduate is to acquire.

Physicians, for example, are said to have "patients." The term conveys a right to expect attitudes that differ from those of a "client." Clients consult; patients are treated. Patients place a heavier responsibility on professionals. Clients might expect to be told what patients might hope would not be told. Are the physicians the school turns out to regard those they serve as patients or clients or something else? What weight, furthermore, do physicians accord a colleague's choice of treatment when they believe that choice counter to the "patient's" ("client's"?) interest? Lawyers know their clients are clients, not patients. But in the adversarial system, they may find themselves in the position of the so-called hired gun. Do they learn the rules of the ABA and the statutes of the state and live by them? Can they live by them without interpreting them?

Three principal modes of forming persons in the professions now present themselves. By concentrating on the job for which the professional gets paid, the schools may produce, even if not by design, manipulators of the profession for their own ends. Or, rather more likely, by insisting also on such rules of the profession as are specifically available, they may work to create functionaries—those who in the social relations of their practice follow the profession's rules strictly and literally and try to behave like clerks even though they will encounter, in a world more complex than a clerk's, conditions they cannot handle. Finally, the professional schools may organize themselves to foster individuals who, aware of the rules and such precedents as are available, grant current practice its weight while entering into the relationships of their profession eyes open to the consequences. They will accept the obligation to make informed judgments.

The first alternative is that of the trade school from which professional schools justly prefer to distinguish themselves. The second is incompatible with the self-consciousness that a liberal education would have instilled. The third alone is consistent with taking professional education as part of higher education. To signal as much, let us call this third alternative the professional mode. It is obvious that not all actual schools at institutions called universities will necessarily choose this mode. But if they are faithful to the interests of their students and of the society, they will.

How are the Models of the professional mode to be constructed? Those professions that deal more directly with social relations, like law or social work or aspects of psychology, will have the means more nearly at hand. Since human affairs are there the subject matter, the network of social relationships aimed at may be worked upon in the very selection of the themes of the professional school's curriculum. Where, as in medicine or engineering, attention falls more emphatically on biological and physical subjects, more reliance may have to be placed upon the ballet itself and upon those chosen for it. In either case, however, the problem of construction of the professional mode must be met, and many professional schools recognize as much.

The recognition, of course, has come in the form of proliferating studies and courses in professional ethics. Two sorts of concern may be distinguished. Faculties and students concern themselves with the way technological developments affect the bearing of the professions upon society at large. The consequences of biological engineering and molecular biology are palpable and great. Awareness of the questions they raise would certainly constitute a major part of that larger context in which the present and prospective aspects of the professional's job come to the fore. Concern may also center upon the social and moral questions that arise for the practitioner in dealing with others involved in the practice—upon the obligations, rights, privileges, preferences (in my formula) that constitute the practice. Professional schools that reject the manipulative and the functionary Models for their people might wish to promote such studies. At the same time, it is doubtful that these would suffice conducted in separation from the other studies and inquiries at the professional school.

There is a reason for hesitating over the practical value of professional ethics. Where the professions are given over to the market economy, the distinctions, uncertainties, and inquiries of the ethics courses can all too easily appear remote. Individuals in the daily round of their activity find themselves in the manipulative mode, where the driving motivation consists in the immediate results: remuneration for skills hired and supplied. At best, they become functionaries observing given rules. As a consequence, the professional mode to which the professional school has introduced its people, tends, despite very different intentions, to become a facade. Taking at face value the account of their future they may have learned at medical school, or business school, or normal school, practitioners claim to serve the public as businessmen or working men do not. They claim to be preeminently "professional," their defining business the service of certain social ends, all the while blandly ignoring any relation of their public ideal to their economic self-interest. Professional ethics, unless profoundly integrated into the functioning of the professional school—how to do that being the distinguishing problem of the professional school—courts the risk of aiding and abetting hypocrisy and self-deceit.

In medicine, for example, the services may be presented as service—free, gratuitous, blue-sky idealism for which the healthy income cannot begin to pay, since for freely rendered service no one can give enough. To show that this is the kind of service they render, physicians then collect their fees through a billing system. In their offices they are grave, paternal, dignified—in sum, disinterested. They are professionals; and therefore bitter at losing that public respect they perceive to be their due and resentful of the public attitude toward their income.

But whatever the pitfalls, the professional school's commitment to the professional mode stands. It can be to the self-interest of none to deceive themselves about what they want. In the interest of their students, the schools must commit themselves to a clear perception of the structure of their profession and of its alternatives. This may not prevent them from deceiving others. But it might prevent them from taking themselves in. We have touched the limits of the coherence Model at which professional education at the university aims.

We have seen in broad outline how individuals may find presented at their professional schools Models of themselves in relation to others in the practice as well as Models for the job itself and its significance—Models of person and of function outside the university. Still, to leave it at that leaves a significant gap in the account. For there is a professional education that culminates not outside of but within the context of higher education: the education offered in the graduate school. We must, therefore, comment on the Models of person and function pursued in the graduate school and on their relation to the self-interest of the participants.

The initial difficulty of the graduate schools in determining the Models that will control their education occurs because two kinds of professions are in process of being prepared for by the graduate schools simultaneously and without distinction. The one is to work as a professional in chemistry, biology, physics, or computer science, or, for that matter, philosophy, literature, or language; the other is to work as an educator in one of those fields. Some professionals are headed for industry, government, or research foundations; others—like those in the humanities but clearly not only those—combine their careers as specialists ("professional" philosophers, physicists, linguists, etc.) with their participation in higher education. Participating is their job—but not their only job. What is to be expected of these two-part professionals? What ought they expect of themselves?

I propose that what is to be expected of them and what they ought to expect of themselves is what they get: conflict. The graduate school faithful to their interests will above all abstain from any move that would eliminate the possibility of that conflict on the grounds that those who do not expose themselves to the tension are failed in advance as faculty members. Not only that. Graduate schools on the proposal will educate faculty for maximum exposure to the incoherence. The schools form the Model both for a role of investigation and for a role of instructor. Graduate students take the consequences of a complex position. That is their right.

The prevailing view tries to reduce the risk and the tension inherent in the complexity by minimizing one part of the role or the other. On this view, the graduate school approximates either a normal school for teachers of undergraduates or a research institute replenishing its ranks. Neither solution is frequently put into practice; in practice, the conflict predominates. But it is felt that something must be wrong.

Those who prefer the first resolution will mark the triviality of most "research." From this observation, and their preference, they will deduce the need to cut down on the requirements for the Ph.D.: first no language requirement, then no dissertation. Or perhaps they will insist upon a separate track for those planning to educate undergraduates. They will complain bitterly that winning a teaching award does not guarantee tenure. They may see the first step in ending the injustice as publicly freeing graduate students of burdens irrelevant to the working life of faculty members.

Proponents of the second resolution will acknowledge the triviality of most (other departments') research and conclude from this that standards ought to be tightened. The Ph.D. is losing, has lost, its meaning. Restore it. The teaching assistant (the T.A.) exists to provide the student with some financial support, professors with more time for other matters, and the institution with cheap labor. Of course, if T.A.'s made a mess of it, they could be dropped, though on the whole they do not seem to make worse instructors than their seniors. The party of original research finds the objective of graduate education to which everything else properly yields in people who locate their professional identity in an active community of scholars: the ones who move from one institution to another, stars.

The chief difficulty of both these positions lies in the inference drawn from them: that teachers and scholars should acquire their own kinds of institution, or either teaching or scholarship should be subordinated, or the same institution should split its graduate school into two administratively united but program-matically separate parts.

The inference does not follow, unless the consequences of not avoiding the duality are unacceptable. It is quite possible to retain the standards of professional investigators or scholars in a discipline while requiring their participation in the educative process. The concern for the making of educators qualified to participate in the ballets of education does not in itself demand curtailing the ability to participate actively in the disciplines; on the contrary, for persons who in the interests of their students are interested in palping and probing their disciplines, such a requirement would seem a necessary condition. On the other hand, nothing prevents the graduate school from making more of its students' experience of higher education than the exploi-tation of their labor. The experience of interaction in the class-room need not be separated from the experience of the graduate faculty who, no doubt, would also benefit by watching the more gifted of their graduate students from whom they also sometimes benefit in their disciplines. The nature, structure, and purposes of higher education are as much proper subjects of the graduate schools as are the professional ethics of medicine or law.

In effect, there is a profession that defines itself by its duality and an education that defines itself by preparation for that duality. Disintegrating the profession and the education would avoid the duality. Still, a unique profession would have been lost unnecessarily. The limitations on student and faculty time and talent no more coerce graduate schools than do multiple course offerings and paper requirements in different subjects. Individual accommodations are a necessary and desirable part of academic life. That students and faculty alike have natural bents that lead them to be happier doing one thing rather than another makes no difference. Obviously, few are likely to be equally successful or happy at widely different activities, and some will suffer for it. Let those who will suffer for it look elsewhere. That is the mandate for any profession.

Very likely, the provision of an education that obliges people to define themselves as subsisting in two communities, that imposes the possibility of incoherence not accidentally but through the deliberate pursuit of multiple goals, will seem like the final letdown of the student interest in coherence. But not so. No one ought presume to guarantee against a need to arrange priorities. In complex enterprises, self-defeat is always on the tip of circumstances. Still, the vulnerability keeps alive the prospect of an altered life, the break in the routine. That is, it keeps alive the gambles of free choice. Having been properly prepared not to miss the complexity, one meets it one's own way, knowing what the options demand.

Let us now return to the relationship of any liberal professional education—professional education is always liberal or it is not professional—to self-interest. That such an education meets the positional interest in effectiveness is self-evident; that it moves toward meeting the interest in coherence follows from the modeling of the individual to the profession's social organization and the needs of its job. I conclude by summarizing the import of the liberal professional education for individuals when the focus of their attention moves from their activity to themselves.

Having gone through the various dances of the ballet, shaped others, and been shaped themselves, encountered and discarded various options, forgotten more than they remember, the educated now prepare to enter into the life of the community not only as receivers of benefits but also as contributors to its life. In that sort of participation, which includes in an essential way the sharing of burdens, the doing of one's part is one's maturity. So a primary benefit of the professional education from the human point of view, aside from money and prestige, is to be tied down and tied to. We acknowledge the pull of such ties when we say,

"I am a lawyer, professor, physician," and mean "That is what I have become, that is what makes me what I am" rather than simply "This is the job through which I get this and that." A professional education that is a part of higher education is finally an education in being.

The dissociation of work and self, therefore, marks the failure of professional education. It is the same failure that occurs in the dissociation of citizenship and self-interest, or in the separation of high-mindedness from "mere" self-interest. For the separation renders the relations that matter among selves instrumental, while reserving the noninstrumental relations of civilization for the attenuated, private, and withdrawn self. The acceptance of that separation would make professional education virtually indistinguishable from vocational education aside from the greater demands of the former on time, money, and ability. The egalitarian point of view that places all occupations on the same level has limited the possibilities of human self-formation.

Perceiving professional education as an aspect of higher education—more specifically, of liberal education—most educators will recognize that their future professionals will be practicing arts, not simply rendering a complex and valuable service through application of acquired knowledge to persons and their situations. The idea of "applying" fails to convey in the present context what the "application" implies. For it implies not primarily a logical or inductive application of what was acquired in law or medical school (although of course there is nothing without that) but a use of judgment in relation to the needs of other selves and their situations. Judgment commits the individual. The individual's judgment is entailed, his or her gamble, his or her intuition—finally, what the person has come to be—in the interconnection with other selves. The exercise of judgment marks and makes the person; judgment is always mine or hers or theirs; it brings the individual directly and incontrovertibly into the process of service. Professional education works for it in the compass of its specific domain.

It is important to be explicit: the professional education that takes the liberal direction determines, along with the self-identification and the self-involvement of its people in some role, what they shall want. This last is basic to the self-interest of individuals who need to know what they shall want, not simply as an instrument to secure what they already want, but in the deeper sense of fixing on that for which they want what they want. The "I" that knows itself a professional conceives its wants as doctor, lawyer, engineer, professor.

To be sure, sometimes those who do the business of the profession and conceive themselves professionals in the accidental sense that it happens to serve their purposes might do a better job than those who conceive themselves as members of their profession. Their success, however, is a success in a skill. The success in knowing what *to* want has been achieved when failure on the job is taken not merely as a mistake in judgment for which one is perhaps irritated with oneself but rather as a violation, large or small, of one's specific commitment; and one pays a penalty in self-esteem. Now success gratifies not only for the sake of something else but also because one approves of oneself for just that success. A liberal professional education has, in a word, made the question of what one wants a question of the location of conscience. Conscience, along with the ability to act effectively as more or less of an expert in a certain field, is the prime business of a professional education that seeks the liberal service of the self.

So there is an answer to those academics in the humanities and pure sciences who wonder what place professional education (except for their graduate programs) might have at a university devoted to higher education: they are taking the professions as a species of overly exalted vocation. If this discussion stands, the choice of professional education by the university committed to higher education is the right one, since education in the professions carries further in the very pursuit of effectiveness the full range of positional interests in higher education.

Chapter Ten

The Opening of the University

WHY NOT NOW, having commented on the nature of the choices in higher education as we find them, summarize and put an end to it?

The walls of the University are not constructed in cement; the boundaries change, the walls are breached, histories are real. (The term "university," capitalized, designates a university or any other institution of higher education.) The positional interests of effectiveness, self-formation, and coherence, which collectively define the self-interest of individuals within higher education, demand adjustments. The interest of effectiveness in a changing world requires unexpected ventures into the broader society outside the University, self-formation a closer involvement with that "outside" during the very period of education, coherence present involvement in the changing of the social world.

The positional interests aside, there is hardly any choice but for institutions of higher education, and most particularly for universities, to move on beyond accepted limits. Government, business, and society in general impose upon them ventures and compliances many of which they are largely powerless to resist. Therefore, they will not resist, not for the most part, not for long. Hence, a problem arises: what to do about social interests other than those the professions serve while surviving as institutions of higher education? On the pretty obvious assumption that cutting down on the "multiversity" poses the problem, not the resolution, the guiding principle might well be one enunciated by William James a long while ago: "Invent some manner of realizing your own ideals which will also satisfy the alien demands—that and that only is the path of peace!"[1] That, when one can manage it, is also the rational path to realizing one's ideals in the face of "alien demands" that cannot all be denied. The University opens voluntarily toward other social interests. It "co-opts," in defense of its identity.

This chapter and the next consider the opening of the University toward work, service, art, and politics. Not every institution of higher education can take advantage of every opening. The thesis, nevertheless, is that each opening serves, in its particular way and suitably constructed, the positional interests of the educative process. Nobody is expected to follow through on all; no one is expected to make work, service, art, or politics the equivalent of a profession. That would mean surrendering, not opening, to other interests. But for those institutions able to take advantage of them, what would such openings be like? What would be the constraints on them? In what sense, finally, would they constitute a legitimate choice for an institution of higher education serious about satisfying the positional interests of students and faculty?

"Work" here consists in participation in the system of exchange among free individuals of their labor. One takes a job, one quits or is fired. One offers a service for a quid pro quo and gets it or not. Professional education already achieves the opening toward some forms of work. There the opening is universally accepted. No one judges the preparation for entering the system of exchange a betrayal of higher education. But if professional educations are not excluded from higher education because they prepare for work in the broader society, the question arises why forms of work other than those of the accepted

professions, which I shall call jobs, might not be introduced in
a suitable way into the conduct of higher education.

Some will ask whether I would actually want to introduce
vocational education into the University. I would not. People
mean by vocational education precisely the education—the
"training"—that neither asks of nor gives anything to higher
education. Obviously, it has no place there.[2] My point is not
that the University have people learn truck driving or clerking
or word processing on campus but that it introduce what has
been experienced in jobs, none of which are undertaken at the
time as life careers, into the experience of higher education.
Jobs would be placed within the context of suitable disciplines
and combinations of disciplines and such readily provided information as the jobs might require would be provided. What
this entails will be discussed in due course. In the meanwhile,
let it be emphasized that the opening toward work entails the
doing of jobs by students in the course of their career in higher
education, not just their accepting the necessity of working in
order to pay for that career.

It will be objected that extending the opening toward work
hardly comports with the purposes of higher education, that jobs
other than professional ones are too trivial to warrant attention,
too simple to summon forth the full potentialities of those qualified for higher education, or too unpleasant. One remembers
the tramp on the assembly line in *Modern Times*. But, of course,
the idea of an opening toward work in higher education is not
to offer people unnecessary preparation for the miserable tasks
in life or even for the tolerable ones. It is to grasp what it means
for most people to become themselves in any society this side of
Eden and the importance of that grasp for higher education. Because the idea of an opening toward work of the kind proposed
here would seem almost trivially obvious if it were not assumed
that jobs other than the professions warrant only the inatten-
tion of higher education, the grounds of that assumption may be
worth disputing.

First it is assumed that the problems of life on the job are, for the powerful minds of the highly educated, routine and dull, since the measure of a problem's interest depends upon its more abstract aspects rather than upon the different kinds of adroitness, skill, perceptiveness, and, indeed, "intelligence" that the problems may call for.

Obviously, there is more than enough routine and boredom on any job. Still, the complexity and difficulties of the "simple" life are underestimated only by fools and the privileged. It cannot be opposed to the interests of higher education to expand the range of application of its sensitivities and attitudes. One ought to note, also, that professionals, to whose preparation few seriously object as a part of higher education, by no means encounter only difficult questions in their practice. The problems that most face are pretty much routine or they couldn't survive. The more difficult ones of law and medicine often either get bounced up a chain of referrals or go unrecognized. Courses in law, medicine, or engineering may indeed constitute in large measure obstacle courses. But the student's ability to surmount the obstacles need have only occasional reference to the needs of the practice. If the demands of the work to be prepared for are the criterion, higher education goes in for a good deal of overkill.

The allied notion that education ought to prepare people to make use of their full potentialities and that, therefore, nonprofessional jobs are infra dig, also runs into difficulties. Everyone has all sorts of potentialities for all sorts of things, even within the context of the University as it currently is. The question is always which are to be realized, which kinds of talent, intelligence, sensitivity, and so forth. Deciding what potentiality to realize, as unhappily every student knows, is not done by deciding to realize one's potentialities. Even if, furthermore, professional education and the life that follows do realize the preferred potentialities to a higher degree, it remains unclear why one must necessarily therefore prefer them to simpler, less demanding work. Perhaps it would be to the self-interest of students not to prepare themselves for the seventy-hour-a-week job in a top law firm for which their talents qualify them. Few, probably, would think it necessarily to their interest to be used, or to use themselves, to the hilt, except for rewards like money and social position.

But a deeper reason still underlies the a priori objection to the opening of higher education toward work and goes some way toward explaining why the other reasons are advanced. An evaluative orientation characteristic of certain kinds of social order is presupposed, one shared by Marxists and members of the happy, workless classes alike.

Marx argued that a capitalist economy dehumanized human beings by reducing them to mere tools and that it achieved this unhappy result through the development of the division of labor.[3] In the interest of humanity, therefore, he and Engels urged a society in which all turned their hands to whatever required to be done. No longer defining their social existence in terms of a job, everyone would have become free for the achievements of civilization. The advance of technology would make it feasible. The capitalist economy ended, there would be work without jobs. Socialism would have transformed society into the University of Vocation-free Education. Institutions of higher education that accommodated in any way for jobs would betray, besides socialism, the high culture and human freedom of which they accounted themselves the agents.

Ladies and gentlemen also regard jobs as degrading, though, unlike Marxists, they consider themselves justified in enjoying both the fruits of labor and their exemption from it. War, politics, and the Church—for all of which higher education is conceived appropriate and even necessary—are placed outside the system of work. Professionals become ladies and gentlemen by dissociating themselves from that system, in part through their involvement in higher education. All live tied to nothing but their own sweet will except for the not necessarily unimportant obligations of their social class—obligations that, for the professionals, are defined by the rendering of specific sets of services. The Marxists, then, in their historical materialism, have merely added that all men are to be gentlemen and all women ladies— free men and women, all joining in whatever needs to be done and devoted to self-realization in culture.

Now our argument for the opening toward work rests neither upon the acceptance of a system of privileges nor upon the demands of egalitarianism, but upon two assumptions. The first, not likely to be contested, is that, regardless of how the content of work may change, the division of labor constitutes an ineradicable feature of any modern economy. The second is that an acceptable alternative cannot be found in democratic humanism; the possibilities of the liberalizing of work are severely limited. Upon this second assumption much of the point of the opening proposed here depends.

Democratic humanism, counterbalancing the Marxist approach, sees the path to the work that frees not in the escape from the division of labor but in the reconsideration of work itself. Freedom now lies in the compatibility of worker and work. "To find out what one is fitted to do," wrote Dewey, "and to secure an opportunity to do it is the key to happiness. Nothing is more tragic than failure to discover one's true business in life, or find that one has drifted or been forced by circumstance into an uncongenial calling."[4] He goes on, "Plato laid down the fundamental principle of a philosophy of education when he asserted that it was the business of education to discover what each person is good for, and to train him to mastery of that mode of excellence, because such development would also secure the fulfillment of social needs in the most harmonious way."[5]

The radical limitations of the system of work with respect to satisfying individual needs make the Deweyan position, benign though it is, inadequate to the business of education in general and particularly inadequate to that of a higher education moral enough to aim beyond a privileged few. Nobody, to be sure, can find fault with happiness or finding one's true business in life if one has any. (Most of us don't; we get by, more or less.) It seems equally incontrovertible that no preestablished harmony exists between the jobs that need to be done in the division of labor and the distribution of persons with determinate and specific potentialities that will satisfy the requirements of those jobs and provide them with the key to happiness. So, if higher education itself has a job to do, it will no doubt seek to prepare those who know what they want and who can find it within the province of the University to attain their objectives.

Yet college and university may have a broader end: to recognize the present reality of the lives of those mired in the system of work by bringing those lives, in their concreteness, within the circle of the participants in higher education. In that way their people go a step further toward learning who they are, and the very incoherence between their lives in the usual routine of the University and the routines of their jobs in the marketplace will constitute a first step in confronting the predicament of their society and of themselves as members of it.

I emphasize that such an opening toward work is to be achieved through acquaintance, not description, so that the individual through a variety of experiences introjects in effect a Model of what it would mean to work in the various enterprises of society that do *not* meet Dewey's criteria. That is why the complexity or simplicity of the job as such is not the decisive issue for the opening of higher education toward work. At the same time, the work the institution finds place for had better be bearable or no opening of higher education toward work will have occurred, only revulsion. The job—or, preferably, jobs— students ought to experience will follow from their talents, tolerances, and situations, on the one hand, and, on the other, on what the resources of the institution permit to be made of the experience.

An opening of sorts has of course already occurred for college and university students. Obviously, if they had any choice in the matter, they would choose only those forms of work that would make them rich, famous, and sexually irresistible. But, *faute de mieux*, they choose whatever they can get. They need the money; they are on the market. Typically, they use the job for a short time for their own purposes and then move on; typically, they go from one thing to another, sampling more or less at random the portions of the map of the economy available to them. They are in a position to regard the job in the light of an exchange that they enter upon provisionally rather than as a self-subjugation of the sort that bothered Marx and Engels when they held forth against the division of labor. They can, sometimes, watch themselves in relation to others, observe what their labor amounts to, and figure what they might expect if they hung on. The institution, however, taking their outside jobs as lamentable but necessary distractions, perceives the gap between work and self-formation in education as unbridgeable. It does not, for the most part, consider the possibility of turning to some use some of the consequences at least of the all but impossibly high cost of higher education.

So we come to the institution's use of work and how it takes part in the opening toward work beyond counseling and assistance in the securing of jobs upon graduation. The use, of course, will consist in turning the experience of work to the purposes of the positional interests. And the institution will do so, to use James's expression, by "inventing" some project in virtue of which the experience becomes relevant to the ballet of higher education, its style, themes, and dancers.

First one must note the possibilities of a more or less varied experience of work that might be relevant to higher education. Work brings to the fore, as the democratic tradition insists, talents and sensibilities of very different kinds, not all of which by any means are invoked by academic concerns. It has sometimes been thought that the business of higher education in a democracy is to cultivate these talents and sensibilities within the college or university. This is not my proposal. The list of abilities is long; higher education cannot take the place of society. But from that it hardly follows that in order to open toward the possibilities of work the university must become the field of work or of preparation for it. What matters for higher education is the encounter of the student with the potencies that lie outside rather than the postponement of the event to a kind of postnatal period.

A second set of possibilities exists. Not only do jobs employ talents and sensibilities outside the academic compass for the opening toward work to recognize. As already suggested, when democratic optimism has abated and the economy has been confronted as it is, jobs are also seen to blunt and destroy talents, to create insensitivities, to employ insensitivities for ends inimical to the human beings who make use of them. Hurts and frustrations mark the conditions of life in the market, not all of them the consequences of the ill luck of the individual; some stem from what the work entails for almost any one under the conditions of the work. What they are, how people deal with them and how they deal with people are outcomes that higher education pushes out of its field of vision to the disadvantage of those it thus deprives.

The University may foster the interest in self, therefore, by the way it proceeds to enter into students' comprehension of what they have experienced in the work undertaken. Understood in the context of higher education, work may cease to appear as a life from which the engaged individuals conceive themselves apart. It may become something they appreciate having experienced because it makes them realize what they are escaping. The slow disasters of the job, instead of leading them to self-congratulation on how lucky they are, might, with guidance, lead to sorrow and concern for those trapped as they are not. There is a difference between existing toward others and excluding them, a critical difference for the making of the self.

But I do not wish to stress now the ethical import of the opening toward work. I do wish to emphasize the significance for the formation of the self in the active participation in the common lot. Whatever ethical code one ultimately comes up with, the entry into work transforms the cast of characters in relation to which one becomes what one is as a mere description of the cast could not. The description alone would still leave the self on one side and those described on the other. The unavoidable task for self-interest is to define the community in which and through which to define oneself. If a higher education is not relevant to that question of the relevant community, it is a good question why it is higher.

It will be asked what higher education can be expected to do about work besides permitting it or encouraging it. Generally, what is to be done will depend upon the choices in the exchanges of the ballet. The primary participants would, of course, be those at the institution with experience to bring to the exchange—the students. But it is vital that they not be the only ones. Though they are at once the primary beneficiaries and contributors, there is no incorporation of their experience within higher education unless there are others through whose intervention the experience appears in a new context and throws new light on that context. Jobs are the topic; but the work experience must be examined creatively. The various professional schools, the humanities, all have faculty—psychologists, historians, sociologists, economists—interested professionally in different aspects of work in the shared society, quite aside from their mission as instructors. These, in their agreement and opposition, their missing of one another and their meeting, will effectively generate the themes that will organize the experiences of their people.

The themes they come up with will assuredly go far beyond the immediate experience of the students and for that very reason offer a context for the student to warp in relevant ways and to be warped by. Contexts altered, the imagination of reality suffers a sea change. Social commitments alter in consequence; and one might expect as well a fostering of creative work in the participating disciplines. In such a way, the more established expectations of higher education are met in the process of working with the active lives of individuals.

Intervention such as I have just described no doubt sounds like a hodgepodge. In a sense it must. To attempt to organize the vast variety of apprehensions and information faculty and students would bring with them would be to assume what is necessarily their task; the openness, the exploration, is everything. Still, the intervention itself must be differentiated from a kind of interdisciplinary program run amok. The experience of the student provides a focus and an ultimate criterion for relevance and irrelevance. If seminars develop for the opening to work, different seminars may develop, different combinations of faculty and students. Tutorials are possible, branchings out from one thing to another as the logic of the enterprise requires. Questions about course credits or graduate requirements, along with most others, must remain open for the good of the program, although excessive formalization of the academic conduct of any opening toward work would probably destroy it.

"Services" are participations in a system of gifts within society of individuals to individuals or of individuals to groups. Because they occur as participation within a system they differ from acts of charity. Because they occur outside the economy or the system of exchange, they are not part of the system of work. They are outside the economy even when they entail the performance of jobs and work to the advantage of the economy. People who minister to the health of poor persons may be performing services despite the fact that in the long run their labor may assist the economy. When society provides the means, like the minimal salaries of Peace Corps volunteers, for the provision of services, those means are to be understood as making possible the giving of services, not as in exchange for them. Anyone, finally—professionals, entertainers, plumbers—might perform services. It is not the intrinsic character of the activity that makes a service a service, but its occurrence within the system of gifts.

The services for which an opening of the University is proposed are gifts of people's time and attention—gifts, as people say, of themselves. The problem of the University is to find a place for the system of gifts in the organization of the campus and to provide a context for the experience of the student within that system as it finds a context for the experience toward work when it opens toward work.

As things now stand at the University, services are typically rendered in an ad hoc way—so many well-intentioned activities, like teaching in literacy projects, performed by persons who are students but not by students as students, even if their institution seeks to give them some support. But preparation, for example, might be called for, and the service directed, if undergraduates are not to make nuisances of themselves in worthy causes. Like the professions, though undoubtedly in lesser degree, and unlike most forms of work, where whatever on-the-job training was required would usually be supplied as a matter of course, the services might well require the ministrations of faculty—in psychology, sociology, political science, and so on—to ensure adequate performance. Schools of applied social science might arrange for programs directly supporting students and faculties engaged in services. In that way, the University, not just individuals connected with the University, opens toward service.

The primary objective of the University must remain, however, the education of its people. While an opening toward service would to a limited extent underwrite the system of services, the opening must reflect back on the life of higher education if it is to constitute an integration of service into higher education rather than the undertaking of new sorts of social tasks. That reflection back will occur for service, as it did for work, when faculties reorganize themselves for the sake of providing an opportunity for comprehending the experience. Only then will the institution have opened itself toward service.

What, specifically, is in this for participants? Individuals enabled to enter the system of gifts return better able to participate in the system of education in a significant way—in our shorthand, better able to achieve their positional interests. Their experience of service affects their interaction in the educative process, their ballet is altered by the facts of their acquaintance. But more: just as the integration of the enterprises of work made possible the perception of work independently of the personal fate of the individual, so the experience of service may be considered independently of the personal goodness of the server. Feeling is desentimentalized; and this desentimentalizing of feeling enables higher education to meet its obligations in special ways.

To begin with, the system of exchange involved students in the system of rights; it involved competition and the securing of ends through cooperation. There were rules to be followed and persons to be granted the same status they asked for themselves. To this extent, they were prepared for the society they were eventually to enter as well as for inquiries in which those relations were essential concerns. The involvements of service, however, differ from those of exchange. The system of gifts involves students in what I may perhaps call the system of supererogation—the structured social arrangements for activity involving other persons and their predicament.

The system of supererogation calls for finer, more specific, and spontaneous adjustments to others than the system of rights. Both are essential parts of a civilized culture. But the system of supererogation, entailing for its functioning a constant perception of the particularity of others in the meeting of their needs, socializes the individual more profoundly. Interpersonal relations become, precisely, interpersonal—relations among individuals in their personal requirements. The very process of forming the relations of service involves a particular degree and kind of awareness both for the one serving and the one served— awareness of themselves not as game player and rule follower but as a "this person." Failing this, what began as service ends as a job, and the server in serving thinks himself exploited.

Accordingly, the opening toward service offers those who take it a way of grounding themselves in the performance of acts in themselves supererogatory and, in consequence of their interpretation within the life of higher education, informed by a knowledge of the world and its possibilities otherwise beyond the individual's reach. That people will take advantage of this option in varying degree and frequently not at all is obvious enough. But no one, I think, can deny the option itself is an option of the civilized society to the purposes of which higher education is allegedly dedicated. Only those will take this education as itself supererogatory who have convinced themselves of the separateness of the intellectual life on one hand and the moral and aesthetic life on the other.

By the opening toward the arts I mean the opening toward the actual doing of the arts by students and faculty, not the attempt already discussed in connection with the study of literature in liberal education critically to appreciate the arts. Moreover, I mean to include in the arts not only the traditional fine arts, but those objects and ways of making objects which approximate the condition of the fine arts in what they produce and their ways of producing. Exactly which "arts" these would be falls outside the scope of this discussion. But photography, weaving, pottery, and the like would be obvious candidates for our attention here. People of some sensitivity and skill work in them and produce objects that require roughly the kinds of approaches that the so-called fine arts do.

The study of the products of at least some of the arts is already an acknowledged concern at all institutions of higher education except the most specialized. One reason is the difficulty of conceiving a civilization of any sort that lacked them. Another is that the arts are among those activities that define the culture independently of the economy and its necessities, which to the intellectualizers is an excellent recommendation. Even so, it is the *study* of the arts in its various forms—scholarship and criticism, history and appreciation, sociology and psychology—that constitutes the acknowledged concern. The place of the *practice* of the arts is more ambiguous.

An English department may hire a writer in residence and offer a course in short story writing, but this is peripheral; its offerings will still center around the usual academic studies and the effort, demanded by other departments, to teach literacy. Music departments may provide for both the performance of music and its study, but the performance is on the whole separated from the appreciation or musicology offered the bulk of students. The best example of the venture toward the practice of the arts may be the drama department. But it is often unclear whether the primary opening of the institution of higher education in that case may not be the opening toward entertainment. In general, then, higher education draws an uncertain line between the practice and the study of the arts that the opening toward the arts attempts systematically to breach.

The line, some may think, is only properly drawn. "There is in art a principle radically opposed to the principle of the academy," Jacques Barzun has remarked. "Between the two there can be only a *mariage de convenance*, which turns out to be one of great and perpetual inconvenience." One gathers that the opposed principle is the "creative," which is difficult to judge, whereas "in academic scholarship or science, technique suffices and questions of doctrine or tendency rarely interfere with a fair judgment."[6]

Barzun thinks artists are better off at conservatories, and perhaps persons out to be professional artists are. But it is the opposition of the principles of art and the academy to which one must object. The notion that in the academy technique suffices and questions of doctrine do not interfere constitutes a very good reason for the rejection of the merely "academic," not only in the arts but in most domains of intellectual activity. Far from being a reason to keep the practice of the arts out, the alleged opposition is a reason for bringing them in. In the liberal arts and sciences, technique (happily) does not necessarily suffice, doctrine is an issue, effective proofs are at a discount. Such, at any rate, is the position required by the present account of the liberal education and its ballet.

Part of the reason for Barzun's line, then, aside from the fact that he seems to have in mind gifted and absolutely devoted artists rather than amateurs, may lie in the traditional assumption that the arts, while subjects of reflection and inquiry, do not afford relevant Models for people engaged in higher education. Artists are inspired, unique, unlike other people. In their relation to the rest of us they are accorded the status of speciality producers offering consumer goods for refined customers, with the participants in higher education on the customer side of the aisle. Critics and scholars become the analogues of the staff of the Consumer's Union—they discriminate for the uninformed what's going on, they say what is to be expected of that sort of thing, and rule on who is truly inspired. (Also, it cannot have escaped notice that all cultures have art, some of it quite excellent, and not only those with a developed science, technology, history, philosophy, and so on. So if higher education is dedicated to a high civilization, the thinking may go, perhaps it would be best to leave what is not correlated to a high civilization to appreciation.) Refinement, not creativity, now marks the educated mind.

The opening toward the arts proposed here, however, follows the precedent of the sciences and the professions (and the precedent of the openings toward work and service, when those openings are accepted). One can imagine what science faculties would say to a proposal to have the University, in dealing with the sciences, deal with them as it does with the arts.

All students, or nearly all, are supposed to have some elementary experience in doing math or physics, and rightly, since the alternative is knowledge of information, not of the sciences. In dealing with the arts, we have made exceptions of them and compensated them with glamour. Yet more people might get the drift of an art and of the arts through participation than are likely to get the drift of math or physics by working problems or repeating other people's experiments.

I propose, therefore, not that every or any student be turned into a professional artist, but that in the interests of the arts and of higher education colleges and universities follow in the arts the precedent of the openings toward work and service, that they make appropriate preparations for the involvement of students and faculty in the activity and seek to infuse that involvement with significance within the established body of higher education. For this end, I make the following modest proposal—modest only because the bases for the opening toward the arts already exist in the current practices of college or university to a considerably greater degree than they do for work or service.

First, let institutions of higher education in the interest of their students, of their faculty, and indeed of their own liveliness, see to it that undergraduates at least do their stint at the art of their choice. Let people in the course of their education dance, sing, weave their tapestries, sculpt, draw, paint, photograph. Let them not merely attend exhibitions or concerts or ballets or theaters or discuss them; let them participate directly in some of the activities of their "higher" civilization. Let them begin to have a perception of what creative activity means. The assumption that most young people capable of a higher education lack any capacity whatsoever to do any art at all simply insults them.

Let it be arranged, moreover, that they work in live relations with others with whom they share the frustrations, excitements, successes, botchings, and strokes of insight that mark the experience of the arts. The sharing is significant; for, it must be remembered, the subject here is art in relation to a social process of education, not to the advancement of the arts. No one would require a professional outcome. Formal credits need not, had better not, be assigned. But work and seriousness would be expected of anyone aspiring to a bachelor's degree and, to make the expectation clear, facilities and instruction would be made available on campus of a kind unavailable for work or service.

The second part of the proposed opening toward the arts requires connecting this doing of the arts to the inquiry into the current state of the arts, their history and place in the community. Here the academic departments of the various arts have a central role: to present the patterns of the history and state of the arts for the student to understand what she is doing and what she is not doing. For the amateur performer, writer, painter, left to herself, everything is fresh, new, and unprecedented. She invents the wheel, often without spokes. But in the study of established and less established works, of good things and poor in relation to one another and in their internal dynamics, students find patterns for criticism of themselves and of their friends and rivals in the associated projects of the campus.

For the departments and their concerns the stakes are high. Their scholarship is invigorated by the prevalent sense of the activity; their investigations are seen in relation to an activity. They are no longer in the corner, on the side. It becomes possible for them to present the work they explore no longer as mere memorials of the past; that past is now. They no longer need present the works to be understood as objects for private consumption, but public objects; their inquiries explicate that public character. Nowhere else in the University can the gap between activity and appreciation, production and consumption, be more systematically and appropriately bridged, given the will to open the disciplines of the arts to their practice. What the strategies of the faculties will be in the process of absorbing the activity before them into their own and their own into the activity before them can no more be worked out in advance for the arts than they could for work and service.

Now we must ask directly what, in the opening to the arts, serves the self-interest of students and faculty. Since asking it that way seems to invite repeating the entire discussion of the relationship to self-interest of higher education, I interpret the question to mean what, in the opening toward the arts in contrast to those toward work and service, would be to the positional interest of those wanting to form themselves and shape their wants. The answer, since the question in effect asks what the self-civilizing mind would find in the arts both practiced and understood that it cannot find in work or in service, or not to the same degree, must plainly be the opening of the individual's sensitivities and understandings to the systems of meaning and consummation that go under the title of "culture." In these symbolic and affective systems, work and service are themselves grasped and expressed; the opening to the arts provides the self a sudden, unexpected life as, through that opening, individuals locate their closest interests. They go public, so to speak, in the act of going private; they find an image of creativity that calls for objectifying the most personal resources of feeling and perception in performance and the grasp of performances. So the self-interest of persons in the arts amounts to the human need for expression in what, in Hegelian terms, would be called the realm of freedom. It is to everyone's interest to be free.

If it be observed that artists have done very well without higher education and professors of art history without doing much in the arts, the answer is, of course, that they have. But the dancers of the liberal education's ballet, having missed the opening toward the arts, have not therefore done that well.

The possible openings for higher education toward work, service, and the arts sketched here have been found justified in the essential concerns of higher education and grounded in the evolving circumstances of that education in the life of the community. As responses to the helter-skelter accretions to the University that have seemed to warrant calling it a multiversity, those openings are at best incomplete. Even so, they may serve to exemplify the kinds of arrangements under which the institution may have some chance of retaining its own integrity when external interests demand their part in the play. They serve, however, as more than exempla. They, and any other openings of higher education successfully realized, broaden the base of community support against the intrusion of interests for which a suitable and proper place cannot be found.

Chapter Eleven

The Choice of Politics

THERE REMAINS A MORE troubling possibility for the opening of the institutions of higher education than the opening toward the arts, service, or even work: the opening for their participants toward politics.

The institutions, at least the most prestigious among them, may already seem wide open. Student protest of all sorts testifies to the politicizing of the University and seems to threaten its very integrity. Interests of race, sex, class, ethnicity demand their part in determining the proper participants in the dance, the proper subjects and themes, the proper styles. Great events like the Vietnam War transform the campus into a battleground; students and faculty have more recently pressured trustees to disinvest in South Africa or to restrict investments to socially approvable corporate activity. Business and Pentagon press for research in one direction or another, and students and faculty alike find it essential to resist.

But while all this represents the rise of political activity on the campus, it does not, however necessary and desirable some of it may have been, represent the opening of the campus toward politics. Political activity is a necessary condition of that opening. But the opening toward politics is a way for the University to employ that activity for its own purposes, not for the ends of the activity itself.

Plainly, as the headaches of the present-day campus show, the politics of concern is an issues politics predominantly, not the party politics of gaining office.[1] That may explain partly why views that often seem extreme to the outside observer or to the faculty member concerned with his discipline are so often at stake, why on the campus political issues are always burning, never just issues. That is why any opening toward politics asks for trouble.

Opening colleges and universities toward politics means not simply converting the campus into a political arena but making political activity on the campus, deliberately and as a matter of policy, a part of higher education. I do not advocate attempting such a course unconditionally; the opening toward politics must be no less tied to circumstances than the openings toward work, service, or art. Passions may make it folly. So may a vast dead sea of indifference. Even so, there is a case for considering the opening as a legitimate and important alternative for higher education even if sometimes that alternative is rejected. The case parallels that for the other openings: (1) made to work, the opening toward politics will be to the self-interest of faculty and students; (2) brought off, it will turn to University purposes an interest that, not so turned, might have made all but impossible the chance of achieving them.

The opening toward politics is more than another alternative. Dealing with decisions on the divisive issues is a matter of obligation for the education that purports to serve the interests of the society. The campus that does not summon its resources to address those decisions may conceivably have served the interests of the economy; but it will have neglected to focus the attention of its own people on the issues of justice and conscience in terms of which they judge the economy and define what they are to want. It will have failed them by withdrawing from their effort to fix their fundamental allegiances as public actions rather than merely private opinions.

In less developed countries, the grave disparity between what students and faculty have come to hope for in view of their education and what they might realistically expect makes them leaders in revolt. Seeking to re-create their societies, they use their positions as students or faculty as a base. Finding little or no movement anywhere to secure the coherence they require between campus and society, they become revolutionaries. Their tragedy—and they may have no way out—is to turn the educative process issue, along with the university's interests in the advancement of science, art, technology, and the professions, into a side issue.

The coherence problem arises as well in more developed countries, though in a less devastating form. As the prospects for effective participation in society improve, women and minorities discover that their chances of securing the fruits of education are not all they would like them to be. Still others discover that they simply do not want what they need to want to enter the economy. In sum, there are those who find themselves more or less left out, those who, as a matter of temperament, refuse to count themselves in, and those who, finding themselves left out, will under no circumstances become part of a setup they regard as opposed to the social good. Each group reinforces the other. Together they make the choice of political action supreme over all other objectives at the institution. I call this the radical response. Change the world. Nothing else counts.

However one may dispute the substance of their proposals, one cannot fairly say radicals have not faced the coherence issue. They have, more or less deliberately, stepped outside their positions as students or faculty and made a political choice: to make use of their positions, if they do not ignore them entirely, for the sake of a greater good. It would be fruitless to argue with their decision by demonstrating the damage to the functioning of higher education.

The "conservative" response to the effect of issue politics on higher education harks back to a time when institutions of higher education ministered to a clientele with relatively good prospects in life. More or less at peace with the world, the conservative finds a sufficient reason for rejecting any opening toward such politics in the disruption of given arrangements for satisfying interests in individual development and careers. Coherence downplayed, politics on the campus appears as closure; any criticism of social institutions must remain within classrooms ideally open to the free exchange of ideas or be pursued under other specifically designed and controlled circumstances for the debate of political issues. Politics intellectualized, observed, and commented upon, the proper participants in the dances of higher education become the Solomons who know all about Sheba but never knew her. Their motto: Let the world alone, change yourself. Let premature participants in the dances of the world practice elsewhere.

Unfortunately—as women, blacks, and the underprivileged, along with new and dislocating technologies and the globalization of the economy, make clear—not all the difficulties of higher education in relation to society are, as the conservative response implies, essentially technical, matters of the more efficient mobilization of means toward acknowledged ends. The ends are themselves the issue. Defenders of the status quo, finding the problems of nonprofessional education less amenable to technical diagnoses than professional, may end up having little use for a liberal education that does not presuppose as the prime directive fitting in or "adjusting." Those among them who nevertheless persist in a taste for the interchanges of that education withdraw into the self-contained worlds of Great Books and Ideas where all coherence problems are logical.

Two responses to politics on the campus, then, tend to dominate the field: the radical response that, recognizing a problem of coherence, tends to undermine the institutional context in which the problem arises, and the conservative that, recognizing the danger to that context, denies the reality of the problem. A third response, however, can also be discerned: Go with the flow; let politics in when you have to; when you don't, keep it at arm's length in political science courses. Those who accept this third response conceive themselves realists. For them, it would be absurd to deny that the choices of higher education must take the limits of action in a world they never made into the most serious consideration as they try to stay afloat. They might even recommend as much to radicals and conservatives and call their recommendation practical wisdom.

The opening toward politics proposed here does not call for "spineless" realism. (For conservatives and radicals, always highly principled, realism is invariably "spineless," on principle.) Since fidelity to the interests of the participants demands at least the attempt both to acknowledge the coherence problem and to save the education, a more appropriate response would seek to determine how systematically to counter the radical and conservative challenges rather than yield to one or the other depending on the necessities of the moment. Granted that the positional interests are—like interests anywhere—potentially in conflict, the response makes arrangements to recognize and provide for the divergent interests within the schema of the University; it seeks to follow James's advice and, in effect, to finesse the problem to the benefit of everyone. This is not done just because one had better; this is done because it is right and proper.

Making arrangements for the choice of politics on the campus means, for this context, both the containment of political activity at the institution and the deliberate use of that activity for the purposes of the University. One makes those arrangements expecting not a resolution of the substantive problems provoking the conservative and radical responses but a continuous commitment of the institution's resources to the precarious process of achieving resolutions.

Conservatives and radicals both must conceive such a response as a failure in principle indistinguishable from the failure of realism. They see the interest in the name of which they reach their conclusion, and it preempts all other visions. Accommodation, which—in our sense, we emphasize—consists neither in bargaining nor in compromising but in the devising of new uses for the political choice within developed institutions, seems, to both alike, betrayal.

Radicals and conservatives have no accommodative problems. Means puzzle them, ends never. Their wants are fixed. Only external forces defeat them. It is, however, a virtue of a "liberal" approach that it admits the possibility of error, and hence disaster, in the very effort to accommodate. That any arrangement for politics other than its suppression or unqualified acceptance might end in the destruction of the University and the defeat of its participants' positional interests tends to show, not that the pursuit of an accommodation was mistaken, but that it was genuine.[2]

The inevitable risk of error admitted, the University's problem becomes so far as possible to fix the conditions that would reduce the likelihood of disaster, advance the positional interests in higher education, and direct the nature of the accommodation of politics sought. While the tactics appropriate for handling particular cases within institutions must wait on the particular case, it is possible to project at least a general context for the arrangements of an accommodative or "liberal" approach.

That context, which I call the University compact, consists in an understanding, implicit or explicit, among the principal members of the University community. At least partly in place at any reputable institution, the compact is the product of a history of institutional practices. I call attention to it, I do not invent it. Some of its recognized features are these: (1) all participants will give priority over any particular position concerning either the politics of the environing society or of the institution itself to the preservation of the condition of fair discussion; (2) disagreements over the political agenda on which issue will be joined will be argued in the context of a decision structure set up before the disagreement in question arose; (3) the general guarantees of civil liberties in a democracy will be preserved, nor will anyone be read out of the community for the substance of his or her views.

Within such constraints, the opening of the University toward politics becomes feasible. The participants in the educative process will try to institutionalize it by whatever means are available. Since only those will feel bound to comply who make their judgments as students and faculty, every effort will be made to assure that those persons who happen to be students or faculty will see and recognize the importance to themselves of their own positional interests. (That other interests are not finally overriding must, of course, be their own decision.)

The compact's containment of political activity, however, is not the opening toward politics but the condition of that opening. At the heart of the opening as a choice of higher education lie the positive measures for dealing with politics. Central to any such measures, defining and warranting them, is careful and disciplined attention by faculty and students to the vital disagreements in the organization and management of the society. These are not to be put aside as though positions were, from the point of view of higher education, a private matter on which students must individually make up their minds after taking the various courses offered by the college or university. That is to wash out politics as a public action. The effort to reach political decisions on issues perforce demands the effort to achieve agreement with others.

That process of persuasion on political issues is uniquely suited to the process of higher education. If political science, sociology, moral philosophy, economics offer themes for higher education, no one should wish to deny the possible choice of their themes at the cutting edge in current controversy. If there is an argument on campus concerning the proper distribution of women and racial or ethnic minorities in the composition of student bodies or faculty, one might, given the acceptance of the University compact, place the argument in the context of the nation's identity as a nation of persons or of peoples. Such debates can be extended and developed to reach into a great complex of decisions that determine the organization of society. The re-making of the world in its basic constitution or its significant parts *is* an issue, one that grips the passions of the student body and one that provides a natural focus for the passionate concern of students and faculty. There is a larger ballet that emerges now, and the re-making is its theme.

A positive role now emerges for the University when campus life grows slack and self-centered. The institution that chooses politics will raise the divisive issues rather than wait for the issues to strike the campus and divide its students. The University, so to speak, asks for it. It refuses the apolitical peace that is the natural hope of both the academic specialist and the student driving for the big career. These are shown another way, even if they choose not to touch it with a ten-foot pole. The University has acted in their interest; it has opened up another way of being.

Of course, on many campuses, in different kinds of schools, moves have been made, in varying degree and in response to the pressures of the moment, to open the campus to political activity. But I stress that the choice of politics of which we are speaking represents the deliberate move, in advance of necessity, partly to preempt necessity, and in that way to be in a better position to deal with the political issues when they hit, but primarily for the sake of the opening itself.

Though the organization of that opening on the campus can no more be worked out in advance than the organization toward work, service, or art, some of the elements that enter into such an organization are not hard to imagine. There might be, for example, curricula developments within the disciplines that bear upon the issues. New courses are possible; established ones can shift emphases or reshape. Forums for the public presentation of conflicting views might be organized. With the development of political consciousness, faculty and student groups may be encouraged to provide, and argue, agendas. Tie-ins between the more formal engagements of the institution and informal campus activities may be encouraged as faculty makes the effort to ascertain what counts in the climate of opinion. Governance of the institution itself may be considered, and student and faculty responsibility for the internal and external policies of the University encouraged.

Even now, faculty frequently share in that responsibility. But students, if they do, usually participate in a very minor way. Hence a problem arises, to work out a consensus before confusion overtakes the campus on what properly may be expected. Such a consensus might sharply reduce the appeal of the most dissident elements on the campus to the majority of the student body and in that way make all the more feasible the latitude that a democratic community would seek to extend all views.

The implication of the opening toward politics in the governance of the University itself is not a structureless majoritarianism. In a sophisticated democratic order, different provinces are delineated for different purposes, certain areas opened to the principle of majority rule and certain areas closed. There is, in effect, a constitution; but for a constitution, it is necessary to work out a consensus.

The opening toward politics presupposes, furthermore, that persons outside the institution, as well as members, will have rights of public expression within the context of university life. It is not only customary but also essential that the political voices of the larger community be heard. Accordingly, the institution will take steps to secure a fair and lively representation rather than simply yield to demands. And of course, bound by the University compact, those responsible will insist on the right of the outside voices to express views repellent to either a majority or a minority.

A legion of other possibilities for the opening of the University calls for changes in the practices of institutions of higher education. Possibilities exist, for example, for the development of relationships with specialized and differing institutions such as think tanks and institutes to explore a variety of economic, technological, social, and political problems. Universities might both expand their own boundaries and deepen the political activities of their participants by involving them in regular communication with students and faculty of other institutions in which the politics of issues is practiced. And so forth. Not all the possibilities will be worth the effort. Of those that are, not all will be worthwhile under the specific circumstances of particular campuses. The opening of higher education toward politics must be constructed. It is not there to be discovered.

If the political opening must be constructed, it is time to remind ourselves what it must be constructed for, which is the good of the participants in the educative process. In the context of the University, the welfare of society is not the objective of the opening, but the objective is advanced through the involvement of the students and faculty in their attempts to understand and shape that welfare. All three of the positional interests are encountered by the University through that involvement. The interests of a world coherent with those of an individual informed and developing in the life of his or her culture generated the need for the opening in the first place. Now the University brings the problem of the achievement of that coherence to the attention of the University community. Sponsoring it, it sponsors—through the cultivation and examination of political activity and political issues—the effectiveness of its people in the changing of the society. In involving them in the disputes and agreements of a democratic society, it enters them as participants rather than as observers in the community, and so broadens the community in which they may locate themselves. It offers them, finally, a choice of comrades. In that choice they define themselves.

In Max Weber's terms, people may take politics as a vocation, a calling.[3] Accepting the choice of politics, the University accepts the vocation. It plays its part in making citizens for whom the political act will be, more than a dreary sacrifice to a felt (or misfelt) necessity, an act of essential expression. Here, the institution lays down for its people, is a possible way to be; take it or leave it—only note what you leave. To have them see it that way, in full knowledge of what that entails, will be the achievement of the opening toward politics.

There is precedent, both ancient and modern, for the conception proposed here for the relation of higher education toward politics. The conception seems misconceived in principle—I do not underestimate the practical difficulties—in part, at least, because of the oscillations in the contemporary view of higher education between technology at one pole and pure mind at the other, never a stop for politics and the making of the common life. Precedent may lessen the reluctance to consider the opening toward politics.

Wrote Plato:

When we are to express approval or censure of a man's training we correctly speak of one of ourselves as educated and another as uneducated—and the reference is sometimes to the business of a huckster or a supercargo—and of other such fellows of mighty fine education. But our present discourse is in place only on the lips of one who holds that education is none of these things, but rather that schooling from boyhood in goodness which inspires the recipient with passionate and ardent desire to become a perfect citizen, knowing both how to wield and how to submit to righteous rule.[4]

"Knowing how both to wield and how to submit to righteous rule" is surely a state that a higher education might hope to achieve for the benefit of its people and their society. Society at large contributes to that end when, in Dewey's words, it "makes provision for participation in its good of all its members on equal terms and . . . secures flexible readjustment of its institutions through interaction of different forms of associated life."[5] The problem of amending the practice of higher education to serve more adequately the positional interests of student and faculty, which is, finally, the problem of the opening of the college and university beyond its usual limits, has brought us down the classical path to the life of the *polis*. The insistence on the role of active participation in the affairs of a liberal education led to that path in the first place.

Undoubtedly, the nature and meaning of an analogous participation has undergone a transformation over the centuries. We cannot participate in the political activity of our day the way the Greeks did in theirs. On the other hand, we do not need to. We are not Greeks. We may seek, in part through the action of higher education, to achieve what rationality we may under our own circumstances. The "passionate and ardent desire to become a perfect citizen" will then not be restricted to that pursuit of set performances within a conventional round that goes under the name of "civics" and constitutes society's way of crossing itself before the unforgiving reality of its problems. A richer, broader concept of the citizen's involvement is available, one that entails "provision for participation in [society's] good of all its members on equal terms" and "the interaction of different forms of associated life." To that concept of a social ethic in its relation to higher education, we now turn.

Chapter Twelve

Ethics and Education

THE SELF-INTEREST OF THE participants in the educative process
has led to essential choices in the conduct of higher education.
The question now is how that educative process, given those
selfsame choices, leads to the exercise of ethical judgment—
to distinguishing the better from the worse in a certain broad
domain and to acting for the better.

I emphasize that higher education as conceived in these pages
educates for that exercise, not that it suffices. Higher education
is no more invariably successful in this respect than it is in any
other. Moreover, as we have just seen in connection with social
issues, it acknowledges the legitimacy of differences of opinion
and makes the conduct of the dispute over such issues its business. People, finally, do not always act in accordance with what
reasonable people and they themselves would concede to be the
better course.

"Ethics," taken in the Platonic and Aristotelian tradition that
approached ethics and politics as parts of a single inquiry, is, as
Abraham Edel put it, "not simply a separate province in which
the moral consciousness struggles with itself in a fretful effort
to do its duty or conform to law. It is a sober reckoning of
policy in the whole domain of practice—goals of life, and the
types of character they call for both in personal development
and in institutional relations, modes of decision and guidance

of conduct, problems of internal conflict, types of interpersonal relations or association and ultimate reflections on well-being." And, he adds, rightly from our point of view, "It is not surprising that the *Nicomachean Ethics* is sometimes approached as a treatise on education."[1]

In that tradition, neglected as much by those who look to the Greeks as by those who look to higher technology for the choices of higher education, this chapter maintains that a treatise on higher education that accorded with the choices recommended in these pages would constitute a treatise on ethics. What distinguishes higher education from specialization as such is its bearing on the complex questions of ethical judgment under the conditions of contemporary civilization. That it has such a bearing, and that the bearing disposes us toward choosing the better rather than the worse—hence toward "virtue"—I call the ethical thesis for higher education. Even if our politicians, public, and academy for their own purposes opt for the conversion of higher education into an instrument for endless improvements in the wealth and power of the economy, in ignoring to the extent they do any central bearing of higher education on ethics they will have chosen for the outcome of higher education a certain kind of person; hence they will have made a decision fundamental to ethics.

Considering the objections to the thesis that higher education contributes to distinguishing the better from the worse and disposes to action for the better helps, if not to prove the thesis, then to show how it might be held. For people are right to suppose that the University does not educate for any specific set of ethical judgments but mistaken in concluding that therefore higher education cannot in an essential way bear upon questions of ethics and, in reflective people, shape the conclusions they will reach.

Primary and secondary education, the church and the family, it is frequently supposed, instill an ethical virtue. People are ethical or not when they come to college or university. Maybe some need to be reminded of what they ought not have forgotten; still, higher education is held to improve their minds, not their conduct. Indeed, when education devotes itself to letting people know what virtue is and urging it upon them, as many suppose any education producing right-minded persons must, it has become moralizing and indoctrination and no longer, therefore, higher education. Yet I do not therefore deny an obvious truth from which the consignment of higher education to affairs of the mind rather than of conduct is sometimes derived. Basic character traits are indeed formed long before students reach the University. The University, however, fosters the exercise of ethical judgment precisely by presenting individuals with a context for the employment of those traits and with a knowledge of consequences.

A further source of support for the assumption that education for ethics properly ends early on comes from the accepted view that ethical behavior consists in observing certain common rules that are, or ought to be, known to everyone. Ethical decision is easy, given only the will. But it is not easy. While anyone who needed higher education to teach him not to murder his mother would be a strange case indeed and the society that bred him even stranger, still ethical *decisions* do not, therefore, consist in simple compliance with rules. Those who hold otherwise are thinking of ethical behavior when no ethical decisions are required. We do not ordinarily consider a person virtuous because he has not murdered his mother.

Moreover, even those judgments that proceed more or less directly from the rule to the case can be challenged. A doubt of the morality of those judgments may throw doubt on the rule. We may be enjoined to preserve life. But it is at least a question whether those who seek to follow the rule regardless of the consequences are therefore choosing the better over the worse course. Our loyalties may be clear in what they demand, each stemming from a clear rule; but then in virtue of their clarity they defeat us. Conflicts of loyalties and the unending task of assigning priorities to meet new situations or to reappraise the justice of old ones put the force of our rules to the question. All this is utterly familiar. Yet cases like these make the pertinence of a higher education to ethics conceivable.

That higher education can have nothing significant to do with ethical judgments follows also if it is held simply human nature for everyone to be out for number one. The view is popular, perhaps on the basis of an extrapolation from a laissez-faire capitalism. Human beings are thought hard-as-rock competitors for whom the norms of ethics are justified as prudential rules for getting and holding onto what is wanted. On this view, in effect, there are no ethical problems—not because there are no problems, but because there are no ethics unless ethics consists of a set of mandated rules. Except for making clear the terms of the social contract and providing information and skills for getting on those terms what one already wants, higher education's occupation's gone. The interest in self-formation that lies at the heart of the relevance of education for ethics has become meaningless when we are already formed, and that is why the ethical thesis presupposes the thesis of sociality.

Even so, we are not compelled to deny the empirical fact from which the conventional view takes off: that under certain conditions of scarcity, attack, or frustration "human nature" will respond egoistically, no matter the education, and that the chances of totally eliminating such conditions approach zero. Selfless selves are not required. We need merely hold that any rational ethic would limit what could be asked of human beings. Then we can defend the possibility of higher education's bearing on ethics by the ways the facts of sociality determine, within the inevitable limits, what the self wants. What the self wants must be formed within a social context. To the extent social change is a reality, who we are and what we are to want—our self-interest—are never entirely settled. The absolute priority of self-centeredness, consequently, will not do, especially for the self-interested.

But the ethical thesis must confront yet another, more interesting objection. Some people attack a significant relationship between higher education and ethics not because there is no problem in discriminating between the better and the worse (aside from ascertaining the facts of the case and prudence) but because there is: we don't know how to discriminate. In the words of Socrates in the *Meno*, "we shall not understand the truth of the matter [whether or not virtue can be taught] until, before asking how men get virtue, we try to discover what virtue is in and by itself." [2] How can one expect professors of "higher" education who, when they ask themselves such questions, characteristically disagree, to take it upon themselves to lead others to make the right judgments and abide by the norms of ethics? Professors ought to know firsthand that they are no authorities on the subject. Therefore, let them forget ethics and do technology or culture, about which they do know something.

The answer to such a position is essential to the ethical thesis. We do not need to know virtue in and by itself. For we do not invent the decision problem that makes it necessary to distinguish the better from the worse, and, further, we have a present life that gives us desires, a past life that gave us precedents, and a set of complex assumptions that represent the agreements and disagreements of the society in which we decide. We begin with what we are where we are; "virtue" is what we end with, if things work out, going about our choices in certain ways.

First, then, when we must decide between the better and the worse comes the situation. First comes the beggar who stops me on the street. First comes the connection between the welfare of my family and the contribution I might make to a communal welfare. Then I imagine, invent, reinterpret, see what's involved, dissimulate, face up. Is giving the beggar his dollar cowardice or consideration? Why is it more important to me to help my family rather than another, or several others? I don't invent the alternatives ex nihilo. I discern them, I distinguish them; there they are, given what I am. I think of the way I've handled things and what's gone wrong and what's gone right.

So not only is the question given, so is the one who answers; and the one who answers is no standardless individual except for what he or she happens to want as a brute fact, but socialized, accepting of a certain self-concept and a certain history in terms of which he or she determines what to want. In effect, we start with an ethic. Confused and uncertain though it may be, it has its touchstones. Certain sorts of things will not do; certain sorts of things must. Following an Aristotelian line, instead of knowledge of the Good, we might make do with a substantial agreement on the qualifying characteristics of those whose judgments of the better and the worse, though sometimes differing, merit consideration.[3] These will be individuals with certain kinds of emotions and attitudes, a certain knowledge of the world, a history such that, regardless of whether we "know" what virtue is, most would agree that theirs are the actions of persons who are at least striving to be virtuous. We start with an image for ourselves, even if we realize we don't quite live up to it.

Those who satisfy such an image would not, for example, judge the cruel treatment of others in the attainment of ends a minor factor in their decisions. They would seek the mean; they would weigh heavily kindliness and responsibility for others. Settling on this or similar examples obviously involves making ethical assumptions. But we cannot make ethical judgments without making assumptions. In order to assess programs and policies—indeed, in order to argue about them fruitfully—we need agreement on the ethical weight of at least some major considerations. If that principle does not suffice to produce agreement in every difficult situation or leads to judgments that in time we come to regret, that is the risk of ethical judgment. There is no *technē* of morality; it is wrong to hope for one.

Let us, then, call "virtuous" those whose decisions, as they seek to make judgments in accordance with what they finally want, tend to favor the better over the worse according to the implicit criteria of ethics as developed by reflective people of their time and society. Lacking virtue patterns in the sky, they begin with what they have. That is all the educator requires. Even the quests of the dialectic required those who, despite frequent shipwreck in self-contradiction, answered in accordance with their basic convictions.

In general, higher education can bear on ethics because ethics, comprising the norms and the judgments of a human being in a changing society and in difficult situations, has to be made before it can be discovered. Then it is remade. Education pertains through its effect on a context of interpersonal and symbolic relations where one of those relations is the one individuals have with themselves. No fixed species modeled for a specific end, human beings do not have a better and a worse in some set of rules and standards fixed prior to their existence. Hence it is the condition of education in virtue, not its obstacle, that the virtuous state or action resists definition in advance.

James Joyce finished his portrait of himself as a young man with some famous words: "I go," he wrote, "to encounter for the millionth time the reality of experience and to forge in the smithy of my soul the uncreated conscience of my race." Set the business of the Irish aside. That extraordinary enterprise, so out of scale a venture for any one man, even James Joyce, is on my account the proper business and ultimate concern of higher education. The key word, of course, is "concern." For all the resources of higher education, skepticism of its own powers suits it as much as dedication. And "uncreated" is the right word. The new conscience, the new perception has to be "forged"—but the forging is from the materials at hand with the tools at hand. Virtue is made, not discovered; and that serves the educator as the answer to Socrates.

But suppose virtue discovered. Suppose a code. Jehovah laid it down, there, in the Pentateuch. What happens? The commen-

taries pile on, endlessly. Whatever the ultimate ethical constitution or its sources, the judgment that accords with it is always
in medias res. Higher education makes possible the commentary
that the exercise of judgment continues to demand.

I have tried to indicate how and in what sense education in
virtue is possible. Now it is left to say how it might be actual in
higher education; and that entails reviewing how the choices of
higher education made in the positional interests of its participants might lead them to pass beyond the rules and policies of
a customary morality and "forge in the smithies of their souls"
their own uncertain and unfinished consciences. For the openings of higher education, the professions, the humanities, the
sciences, and the ballet that marks them all transform attitudes
and supply a context for the reevaluation of the judgments with
which people start.

First for the most obviously relevant of the openings, the one
toward service. We take the relevance of compassion to an ethical virtue as an initial agreement. Higher education, in making
feasible, in relating and interpreting the acts to which compassion leads, transforms that compassion into a part, precisely, of
the "conscience" of the community. Compassion can now be
seen by the compassionate as part of the conscience of society
rather than as a momentary and slightly eccentric expression of
an impulse or the admirable gesture of a commendable but particular human being. What had been supererogation becomes
obligation, and a nonsentimental humanity becomes, for those
who take the opening, a live possibility.

Of the opening toward politics perhaps enough has already
been said. Certainly, the ideal of the "perfect citizen," perfect in
civic virtue, accorded better with the circumstances of the small
city on the crag in ancient times than with those of the huge,
nested, multifaceted societies in which we live and sometimes
try to act responsibly. Appropriately, therefore, the politics that
is taken into higher education presses upon those who partici-

pate in that education the necessity of resolving the conflicts among the groups to which they and their fellows belong in a wider context, with respect to a far greater range of interests, than they would otherwise attend. At a crucial time and place in life, they seek justice. However driven by the exigencies of where they happen to find themselves in life—black or white, male or female, rich or poor—they would never dream of advancing judgments that stemmed from a drive for predominance. They want, they call for, the exercise of moral judgment. And they are not therefore hypocrites; that is essential. They require justification; to find the justification, to contest it, becomes their business when they accept the opening toward politics. They are learning what it means to do social ethics.

So also does the opening toward work go to "forge" the conscience. Whether that opening is entered upon or not effects the presence or absence of what Judith Shklar calls one of the "ordinary vices," snobbery—"the habit of making inequality hurt." The snob, she writes "while he annoys and insults those who have to live with him . . . injures himself as well, because he has lost the very possibility of self-respect. To be afraid of the taint of associations from below is to court ignorance of the world. And to yearn for those above one is to be ashamed not only of one's actual situation, but of one's family, one's available friends, and oneself."[4] By any account, the tendency to hurt others and in the process to lower one's judgment of oneself must be counted a vice and, under the circumstances of social inequality making for snobbery, the absence of that vice must be counted a virtue.

College or university, however, would not have courted that virtue if financial need alone related students' jobs to the institution. Then the job and those associated with it could well be resented and, in the course of rising in the world, every effort made to pretend the painful association out of existence. Here they are, then, those University men and women, forced to descend to the class below. They must prove the propriety of their membership in the class upstairs; they must associate with that superior class all the more exclusively, dissociate themselves all the more disdainfully from the persons in whose company they lapsed, even though they had no choice. Closed to work, as for the most part it is—perceived and presenting itself as the prime means of escaping low-paid and ill-esteemed social positions— the University becomes the natural hothouse for a generation of snobs.

I do not, of course, mean that if the opening toward work is entered upon people are going to like work. Rather, the life of work understood and grasped in its relations to the possibilities of human beings and of societies, placed as a live activity within the context of the University's attention, ceases to be simply someone else's fate. The opening raises the equal standing of the members of society to the status of a significant problem. For, of course, not everyone is equal to everyone in all respects. How are they equal, how unequal? The rejection of snobbery raises a question of ethics, not a solution. More significantly, the domain of moral sensitivity expands substantially. The doing of the job, demanding actual engagement with persons who live very different lives except for that, engenders the perception of them as fellows when the common fate and the necessity are understood. A common plight, a common end, accepted and prepared for, makes human beings comrades whether they like it or not. They share an immediate response, an immediate recognition of their situation, that inform and give edge even to their quarrels. This apprehension of others, I propose, goes some way toward characterizing the person whose judgments on what is better and what worse are to be taken into account.

The opening toward the arts may seem to have least to do with virtue. Fiddle players are not notoriously more virtuous than others. But then the opening did not aim to make first or second violins in a symphony orchestra. It aimed to provide at least one clear occasion in life in which discipline and expression are united by communal demands of performance. The opening accepted, everybody plays, dances, sings, writes; styles are encountered, used, individuated, congruent themes discovered. The individual experience becomes a social experience and, in consequence, part of the social self. The individual self, seeking to express itself, has been socialized, the socialized self individualized. Seeking after self-expression in relation to others has become part of what it means to lead a human life. It forms what one is to want, shapes one's virtue.

The implication is not that the arts present right ethical judgments. It is that the intense conjunction of personal and social experience in the doing of the arts lays strains upon expectations of self and others, and that such strains lead to new sensitivities and perceptions not always compatible with conventional reality. Dancers in the ballet of the arts travel downtown to Bohemia through no mere whim. However modest the creation and the talent, they take it as their business to make the game they play their own. A touch of Bohemia in the soul is a prime desideratum, though far from the only one, for a more live and sensitive ethic. The consequent mistakes may be preposterous; but to be preposterous is something of an achievement. At least the judgments are the person's own.

The pertinence of professional education to ethics is obvious. Professionals function at the confluence of work and service. That is the source of professionals' typical moral problem. They perceive themselves either as sellers of services on the market or as providers of a service concerned with the norms for providers of that service. Or both.

For questions of professional conduct arising from the point of view of sellers, a code settles the matter. In the entrepreneurial exploitation of their competence, professionals find in that code, which is external to them, a set of constraints that makes their life easier. Referring to the code enables them to go about their business without worrying about difficult decisions. So law schools, business schools, medical schools, and the rest pressed to "teach" ethics, as they increasingly are, are pressed to get their students to accept the conditions that will

make their practices socially acceptable and hence the more
likely to flourish. (If MBAs are taught ethics, there may be in
the future fewer damaging scandals in the securities business.)
Professional schools choosing to serve that perfectly reasonable
end alone necessarily instruct in escaping the exercise of ethical judgment—an escape often associated with the interesting
ethical judgment that ethical judgments are to be avoided by
anyone who knows what's good for him.

When, however, professions are actually conceived as more
than means for personal aggrandizement under the mask of
social service, the problem of professional education becomes to
engender self-perceptions that will make students professionals
in the sense in which one makes a profession: by incorporating
complex norms not simply as rules of the game one is playing for
one's own purposes but as standards for determining one's own
self-worth. The individual now makes a venture into virtue, as
young people in medicine or law frequently become aware when,
feeling themselves at stake, they perceive the insufficiency of
their subject matter, their technology, and their conventions
for determining what in their professional capacities they shall
be doing.

The professional school, then, that takes its education as a
preparation for a profession as well as for a business engages with
its students in determining who they are to be; it constructs
the self-interest of its emerging professionals as professionals by
seeking to establish the priorities through which they will deal
with others and with themselves. Inevitably, it educates for one
kind of virtue or another, one kind of ethic or another. Determining what it means to render service and to look after oneself,
it determines what everyone agrees to be an essential part of
ethical virtue. In none of the conventional provinces of higher
education is the opening toward ethics more direct, more incontrovertible, or more worrisome in respect of its likely upshot
under present circumstances than in professional education, and

this quite aside from such involvements as torts and criminal law in the law schools or medical ethics in the medical schools.

The consideration of the ethical force of higher education leads, finally, to the relevance to what I have been calling virtue of the education that traditionally has made a fuzzy point of promoting "broad" perspectives and "well-roundedness" in behalf of the interest of the individual. I shall try to indicate quite briefly how liberal education, including therein general education, disposes, and might further dispose, toward the disposition of its students to choose the better over the worse.

Consider, first, general education and its maps. The maps don't give detail; they sacrifice it for the lay of the land. In so doing, they provide an account of the primary interests of the society—where those interests are to be encountered, how they work and how one sort of thing tends to affect another. Students begin to learn where and how to look. As they appraise the various prospects and circumstances they are likely to face, they become, in however small a measure, worldly-wise.

Now a degree of worldly wisdom is commonly accepted as a necessary condition for discriminating the better course from the worse. For the immediate choices we make for ourselves and our families, for the avoidance of the more outrageous alternatives in the decisions we reach about the moral issues of our society, the maps of the world that make up our worldly wisdom constitute the indispensable context. To be sure, nobody knows the specific consequences, beyond a very limited horizon, of even our routine choices; often, if one did, one might find oneself the more incapable of choice. Still, we know something, enough to make conjectures. We have this to our credit—that while we know we might have been mistaken, we have avoided folly.

In liberal education generally, the opening toward ethics occurs by indirection: through the ballet, through the Models, through the critical encounter with a wide range of relevant material and experience. There is no alternative, for even if all the faculty's directions were correct and Socrates' problem in that way solved, students supplied with precepts would have received only directives and been left with the problem of what to do with them. The Protagorean problem would remain.[5]

The central point is that one does not "teach" virtue the way one teaches principles; the capacity to distinguish the better from the worse follows from experience taken in a certain light rather as the writing of poetry or fiction does. Nobody makes poets by teaching scanning; people become poets by being what they are and assimilating into their sensitivities a wide range of largely unpredictable experiences. Then they write. And they write in a context of criticism and other writings on which they have reflected. They cannot, literally, be taught "creative writing." Similarly for ethics; liberal education does not teach creative ethics; it bears on a creative ethic because of what it does with other purposes in mind.

In the ballet of the liberal education, the particular stand-points and requirements of students and faculty meshed, con-flicted, and, in the process, were redefined. In this way, the bal-let reproduced the condition of a participatory and responsive social life under circumstances in which experimentation be-came possible without the often deadly consequences of action in the world. Styles of being with one another were engen-dered—styles of humor, of insight, of conflict, which worked to make wants civil, disposed to society, and tractable for ethical perspectives.

One hopes that those who entered upon this ballet would, in a significant measure, have the qualifications to do so before their entrance. But in the nature of the case, the participants would strengthen those qualifications through the dance. The ballet would have pressed them, sometimes against their incli-nations, toward taking upon themselves the risks of their pref-erences; in that way it would have moved them to meet the necessary condition for ethical choice. For there is no ethics without self-determination, no ethics in the more difficult and uncertain predicaments of changing life without risk; and these the ballet fosters in the contested relationships with others and their opinions.

Given the willingness to take risks, when self-awareness is encouraged, when the free, the open education renders palpable the incoherence of what the self wants and what it may expect in the world, it is not accidental that indignation over the injustices and ill fares of society seize the players in the liberal games and that they rebel. That such responses come more readily to students and faculty of the arts and sciences than to those of an engineering or business school testifies to the efficacy of a liberal education.

Turning now to the particular disciplines, we consider first a customary preoccupation of the liberal education, literature. Literature is often approached as either something to enjoy, although of course there is nothing wrong with that, or something to approve or disapprove from a moral point of view. Yet it need not be taken to serve only isolated pleasures or the moral improvement (or corruption) of readers. Literature, taken in relation to the performative Models and not as a collection of documents to be studied and classified, can supply a sense of what it might feel like to be a human being other than ourselves. In doing so, it clarifies what it feels like to be the human being that is ourselves. This is no secret of mine; but grasped and placed front and center, it makes the import of literature for ethics palpable. For it prepares us to treat people, including ourselves, as subjectivities rather than as powers for changing the arrangements of things to satisfy wants. Good and evil are now made flesh and distinguished from the abstractly harmful and helpful. People wildly different from ourselves have become persons. At the same time, the widening of the experience of human subjectivities that literature achieves has widened the set of relations in terms of which we now locate and differentiate ourselves.

That the sciences dispose toward the choice of the better

course over the worse one quite aside from the information they contribute—which, of course, can be absolutely indispensable—I need not dwell upon. Peirce, Dewey, Mead, and others have all made central the importance of the attitude that corrects belief through a procedure that does not presuppose the truth of the beliefs to begin with, that is in a profound sense interpersonal, that insists upon the possibility of error, and so on. An active intelligence stands at the heart of any ethics a secular college or university would wish to foster, an intelligence which, seen at fever pitch in the sciences, might under appropriate circumstances be made effective in domains outside the formal sciences. There is no need to presuppose the direct transfer of experience. The perception of the relevance of science and its perspectives underlies the very concept of modernity, from the Enlightenment on. A freeing from superstition and confusion, a recognition of the need for clarity and of the possibilities of human action in changing the physical and social world, alter the possibilities for the exercise of ethical judgment as much as any specific information the natural or social sciences might provide.

Now, finally, for the place in a liberal education of the direct inquiry into the subject of ethics itself. The emphasis heretofore on indirection in relation to the disposition to virtue was never intended to derogate the role of the explicit and specific analysis of ethical problems in shaping that disposition. The most virtuous persons in the world loaded to the gills with relevant information will find themselves stumped more often than not by the infinite variety of circumstances. Now dealing with the puzzles of ethical conduct becomes, more than an intellectual game, a part of ethical virtue. Only in virtue of the experience of having encountered those puzzles systematically and directly can one finish one's preparation for taking one's stand, whatever it may be, responsibly.

There is no great mystery about what one deals with in addressing the problems of ethical conduct. Certainly, one considers the state of ethical theories, but not to find the premises from which to infer the proper resolution. Any effort to define an ethically justified conclusion by assuming to begin with the adequacy of an ethical theory stymies ethical deliberation rather than improves it; ethical theory, like any other kind, needs to be tested to survive. The possibility of that testing makes moral philosophy possible. At the same time, though theories and their analysis may not be relied upon for answers, they contribute slants, proposals, contexts that may prove illuminating. Nothing new here.

Preeminently, however, to provide the conditions for the exercise of deliberation, one handles real cases, cases, therefore, that are almost always more complex and demanding than set-ups. In effect, one proceeds like the professional schools when they seek to explore their decision problems at the profession's cutting edge. The difference is that their explorations are restricted to the special situation of the profession they serve while what we may now think of as the opening toward ethics in liberal education seeks its cases over the entire field of human experience. In this way, that education enlarges the variety of hard cases, raises alternative ways of handling them, and in general provides a ground and framework for the predicaments of ethical choice.

It would seem, then, that a liberal education has the option of making the inquiry into ethics, more than the concern of a special discipline, namely, philosophy, a common concern of many inquiries. The social sciences and the humanities may be made to reach toward ethics through the choice of appropriate themes. The social sciences need not be pursued only as sciences, if they are pursued that way; they may be seen through their disclosures to raise questions in ethics. History, literature, and philosophy may have another end besides the advancement of their own disciplines. All might sometimes choose to work their materials to express the decisions people make and have made—and not merely to show that they have made them, but to show how they perceived the problems, how they justified their resolutions, and with what warrant, as it seemed to them and now seems to us.

For an obvious example, the study of history includes the examination of the choices people of prominence and ordinary people have made under the circumstances of their lives as they perceived them. Have they, in their own context, made the better decision? Would their decision have been the better one from our point of view? Each question raises its difficulties; the relationship between them throws light on the perspectives of these people of the past and on our own. The sensitivization is all, and achievable through the construction of appropriate themes without any damage to the aim of the historical discipline itself. One studies cases in the justification of ethically relevant decisions.

The same holds for the social sciences that, though often more concerned with the causes of judgments, also deal with their justification. Disciplines like sociology or anthropology might use for themes the problems people encounter in their own contexts of good reasons. They might seek to assess what those contexts presuppose and how fully the presuppositions are grasped. They might raise questions about how social and national predicaments are perceived and resolved. Their value to their students, then, lies not merely in the information or even in the sociological or anthropological truth as such, but in an exponentially increased experience of the difficulties and possibilities of rationality missed and achieved.

Consider, finally, the themes available for the study of ethics in philosophy when that study makes central the general interests of a liberal education. I hardly propose that dropping meta-ethics from the philosophy curriculum will serve those interests. But surely a question of focus and emphasis remains. If the exercise of judgment is the end, a theory of justice will have a higher priority than a theory of language. If they do nothing else, theories of substantive ethics leave students and faculty no alternative but the hot pursuit of counterexamples—hard cases for the theory, hard cases for those who would like to know what actions are morally warranted.

In general, that work in philosophy will best serve the self-interest of the undergraduate which systematically examines the themes of moral philosophy—lying, secrets, confidentiality, for example.[6] While such themes are old in philosophy, they surely deserve the central place in the education of undergraduates trying to discern the structure of their own lives. The liberal education that opens seriously toward ethics, and in that way serves the positional interests of its participants, will, if at all possible, give priority to the substantive themes of moral philosophy in the undergraduate core curriculum.

There is a further move beyond the department of philosophy. A liberal arts faculty and interested elements of a scientific community could make the common object of their joint and separate activities the study of the grounds of ethical judgments and ethical practices. Pursuing such activities and heeding one another in the process, the faculties of those disciplines whose work bears upon the exercise of judgment will see themselves doing their own proper business, not crossing interdisciplinary lines. Dealing in common with a common problem, they will have made a not insignificant choice of higher education, one likely to put off only those who find a liberal education essentially repugnant. Programs of this sort, however, are only possibilities, matters of luck and temperament. As such, they lie outside the discretion of the University.

In summary, higher education *is* education for virtue, which does not prevent it from being education for many other things. In fact, it is precisely through those other things—the various openings, the processes of professional education, the ballet of liberal education in all its phases (including the explicit study of hard cases and what makes ethical justification possible)— that education is education for virtue. Through them it disposes people to exercise ethical judgment by increasing both their ability to distinguish the better from the worse and the likelihood of their acting for the better.

For such a culmination not all the exhortations of academic statesmen would make a difference. What counts is the choices administrators, faculties, and students make in the conduct of their daily operations. The interest in self-formation in the contexts of civilization, the tie-in of self-formation with the interest in effectiveness, and the unremitting need for coherence make higher education's bearing on the choices of ethics inevitable.

In this bearing, we may now add, inheres such unity as may be appropriate to the University. Such unity does not stem from the nature of the subject matter dealt with. Complicated subject matters may be dealt with as complicated puzzles; simpler materials seriously addressed might provide floods of illumination. Nor does it have anything to do with covering a large amount of specific material. Higher education need not be a marathon run for pedants, a culture qualification course for a leisure class, or a preparation of highly endowed brains for the service of a market. Obviously, colleges and universities might go any of these routes. On the other hand, they might seek to remain faithful to the self-interest of their people and pick and choose among their various components by asking which part—which school, which curriculum, which course, which accommodation to the society, which resistance—best serves that interest. In that way, they achieve their shifting identities in the service of virtue.

─────────────■─────────────

Chapter Thirteen

The Choice of Higher Educations

ON THE ASSUMPTION THAT the self-interest of the participants in higher education called for choices that, ultimately, rendered higher education an education in virtue, we now ask why we would want to place the self-interest of the participants front and center. There is, after all, no a priori necessity to construct a University education that insists on satisfying the positional interests that colleges and universities profess for their people. Colleges and universities profess other interests also. They profess to be committed above all to the service of the community. They profess to be fundamentally committed to research. More than anything else, perhaps, the effective commitment of our colleges and universities is to satisfy the general social drive to make out, while self-formation in the context of civilization occupies a back seat. The defense of the choices of higher education advocated here depends, therefore, upon what reasons one might give, what reasons society might have, to justify the choice that committed itself first and foremost to the positional interests.

An ancient argument concerning the higher education to be preferred for the citizens comes to mind. Most of the citizens who attended the Sophists' lectures thought they had a case. They did; wealth, power, position, are indubitable goods. But the question was and remains whether it was the best case. Ultimately, the choice of educations drives us to ask what sort of human beings we wish to work for. The alternatives thrust us back to the kind of virtue we value.

"Despite glowing reports of successful multimillion-dollar fund-raising drives," we read, "many of the nation's top research universities are having trouble sustaining both advanced research and strong undergraduate liberal arts programs," and "As a result these universities, which offer graduate programs and conduct research in a variety of academic disciplines, are breaking up, eliminating or cutting back departments that were once well-regarded." Moreover, "some critics say the colleges . . . have become too attracted to mounting expensive and 'exotic' programs that have drained university resources and obscured growing fiscal problems."[1]

The people who run institutions of higher education disguise their priorities behind the mask of financial feasibility. But these priorities show. Who shall be thrown from the lifeboats? "You. So sorry, we're short on space." The departments and programs not cut or eliminated are most often those with access to resources not generally available to the liberal arts. The cost of research squeezes, not because of the expense of producing advanced work in classics, art history, or philosophy, but because of the great expense of producing that kind of work in those fields that might bear upon potentially profitable technologies. Money does not merely talk; it makes confessions.

It may seem, therefore, that those who do the job of higher education, the students and faculty and those who work with them, have no real choice among the alternatives imaginable for higher education, not when the chips are down. But it does not follow that they are powerless just because, self-evidently, there are other major and more powerful players. They have their own kind of leverage upon institutional policy and public opinion. There is, despite prevailing winds, a certain slack or looseness, a certain possibility of tacking. (In matters of social policy that is all anybody does anyway, if one expects to do anything at all.) In varying degree, depending on the institution, faculty set curricula, determine (in the better schools) their own membership, apply their standards, and so on. Students, given any sort of chance, can raise the devil. If they can be led to see an issue of principle, they often will, for better or worse. Administrators, within the constraints of their particular positions, are sometimes subject to reason. Trustees are often willing to abide, in the interests of peace and the reputation of the institution, what they consider to be a certain amount of nonsense. Faculty and students, after all, determine the reputation of the institution. If having a choice means having the possibility of action, they have a choice.

They have that possibility if—granted the large size of that "if"—they can secure a minimal degree of consensus. These remarks are addressed principally to the consensus of the faculty. As things are, it is the faculties, and within the individual faculties their members, who are divided and conquered as they seek their own specific advantages. Prudence, therefore, recommends that they seek objectives besides their own competitive advantage against one another. Political naïveté, not high intellectual standards, makes the philosophy of education seem an idle distraction from the serious business of pushing an academic career. Faculties must have it out within the constraints of the academic compact and form a context that reflects a common interest. Only a general concept of the business of higher education in which they are all involved will provide such a context, and hence the possibility of reaching a consensus that will enable them to defend themselves against external pressures and internal confusion.

How successful faculties will be in reaching such a consensus one hesitates to say. Still, it helps to realize that some basis for one already exists. There is substantial agreement that the sciences, the professions, and the humanities are all to be taken seriously by a higher education. (How seriously, of course, is a question.) Again, although just what is to be done about it is another story, no one denies a grave necessity to deal with the unremitting efforts of students and their outside supporters to control the offices and membership of higher education and its programs in the interest of competing ethnic, racial, and sexual groups. In a measure, this discussion has illustrated, and recommended, ways of dealing with both these matters.

My concern now at the end, however, is not to offer solutions and strategies for the protection of the interests of the participants in higher education but to suggest the commitments and preferences in terms of which one might want to work out solutions and strategies. I return, then, to the basic question of the alternatives of higher educations in relation to the kinds of person—the sort of virtue—one would prefer. What higher education do we choose? Is it to be one like the higher education described in the previous chapters or some other? Not only faculty but students, administrators, and the general public to which they appeal will finally have to justify their decisions by referring to the kind of society they would choose if they had a choice.

Colleges, universities, and institutes might organize their educations to support either those who, in Nietzsche's way of putting it, give themselves their own law or those who accept the law of others. At the accepted apex of the educational system they might educate for self-determining persons, capable of choosing for themselves the very norms that distinguish the better from the worse or for those often good enough—certainly more reliable, certainly less discomfiting—people who follow rules. To be sure, everyone favors critical attitudes. They protect us against possible enemies; we feel, and are, vulnerable without them. But there is a question of the kinds of critical attitudes one opts for, those that work within the critical schema accepted in the world or those that question it. We aim to be critical of our politicians and of the goods we buy, but not therefore of our political ordering or the priority of consumer goods. We have learned to be suspicious; we are determined not to be hood-winked. But there may be more to critical attitudes than that. There is their employment in the assessment of one's own wants and in innovative or creative action. The institutions that work for one sort of criticism will build one sort of higher education; those that work for the other sort, another.

Higher education might also throw its weight to produce highly useful persons, anything more to be considered culture and therefore disposable. What is highly useful would be deter-mined by the very difficult things most people cannot do and which, it is felt, need to be done, given the wants at any time of the society. That students want this with their whole hearts there is no doubt; they are fighting for their lives and paying dearly. Still, the question remains whether being prepared to survive must imply as its price isolation and deprivation. It may be that, the way things are, the single-minded emphasis on highly useful information and techniques is the most efficient way for students to stake out their space in the world. Perhaps the University will be well advised to help them do what they feel they must; but perhaps not, or not always. How much of their lives will one help students sacrifice for careers? How much is an increase of a degree of competitiveness worth? There is a moral issue here. I do not say it is easy or that we can manage it other than step by step.

A higher education might also, as we have seen, end with persons who passively accept the inevitable requirements of the division of labor and define themselves and their virtue in terms of two separate functions: consuming and producing. To be sure, everyone must accept the products of the work of others and give others their own work in exchange. Still, the question remains whether to assume the separation of the functions as a necessity of higher education or attempt in the educative process to form another image of a human being. Shall the University strive to make its people into well-paid employees of others and, more seriously still, of themselves? This in some measure happens to us all; but it does not follow that we ought to educate for it. My thesis throughout has been that there are choices of higher education that might produce a virtue that puts it to people to choose for themselves the better over the worse. Of course, we do not know the consequences. We live pretty much the split life and find that we can take it. Why not play it safe? There is always an argument for going with the stream.

Higher education does not produce the current; whether its practitioners—its faculty, its administrators, and, in their way, its students too—drift in the stream will depend in the long run on who they are and what they value. These determine their image of the general good; that image in turn will broadly determine their judgment of the constraints on their roles and of the responsibilities, aims, and privileges of those roles. They will have moved toward the apprehension of their proper ethic. If they align their judgment with the choices summarized here as education for virtue, they will have chosen for an "ethic" of higher education a set of professional responsibilities, aims, privileges, and constraints other than the one that now tends to call the tune and promote a very different virtue.

The apparent victory of democratic attitudes over the blundering tyranny of the command economy makes it particularly appropriate to relate the problem of the choice among higher educations to democracy and democratic values. For, presumably, most of us would choose an education appropriate to a democracy. I propose that anyone willing to accept at least some of the principles that are the objects of democratic commitments would be obliged to accept the higher education that made self-formation central.

A democratic order, plainly, requires first a commitment to equality. The question is, on what terms? What concerns us is not majority rule as such; it is the nature of the commitments defining the majorities that determine different policies and the limitations that a constitutional order would seek to place upon majority rule in general. What does the condition of equality demand: the equal liberty of self-formation or the equal service and acceptance of that public opinion against which Mill warned— the service and acceptance, finally, of the market?

People whose education has consisted in the acquisition of very useful skills serve the market that supports them. They accept a uniformity of presupposition concerning what they are to be doing and what they are to be doing it for. Even as the variety of consumer goods that satisfy wants multiplies, the equality of the market standardizes wants. There are simply plural markets, differently priced. The condition of social equality that Alexis de Tocqueville analyzed over a hundred and fifty years ago has been realized, not in terms of the participation he found in the town meeting, but through the growth of mass markets.[2]

So have the risks of manipulation in this country been realized, if not by political despots, then by "the merchants and tradesmen" whom Tocqueville thought must also eventually yield to the people.[3] In part, they or, in our terms, the requirements of business, create markets; hence in part, and in no insignificant part, they create the people. Does the institution of higher education throw what weight it has to the furtherance of that process? This, plainly, the choice of higher education urged here does not do. In place of the individualism of competition for the same goods, it sets up the grounds for the differentiation of goods. In place of the fraternity of resentment, it sets up a possibility of the fraternity of self-determining individuals.

Let us comment further on fraternity, another member of the classic triad. It is often thought that higher education separates people off from fraternity. It need not if it takes seriously the implications of the involvement with one another that the openings toward work, service, art, and politics address. For these entail not only the friendliness of individuals of the same class but also the acceptance and understanding of the demands of the other citizens so that the satisfaction of their wants is perceived as some part of one's own good. Yet a higher education will almost certainly substitute alienation and indifference for fraternity when it devotes itself preeminently to specialized selves and careerists.

A collection of different sorts of successful specialists, moreover, united only by a shared desire for consumer goods (which is not the same as a desire shared) will not constitute a fraternity. For such persons any common life lived outside the partitions of function tends to become accidental, the natural province of the happy advertiser. The separate interests of interest groups supersede it. People have become specialists in action, generalists only in passivity. Certainly, higher education cannot in itself prevent that consequence. But in what direction would we have it move—toward the creation of fraternity, or away? If toward it, toward what exactly?

There is a fraternity for higher education that is not compatible with the fraternity of the democratic commitment. The participants in higher education, inspired often by real grievances, may seek to convert the University into a rivalry of different associations—different bands of brothers, different clans, each doing independently what it finds most useful to its own consolidation under the University roof. Affirmative action, women's rights, and so forth, are not in themselves the issue now, but whether, when these are sought, they are sought to heal past dissociations or to preserve and build higher walls still. It will not always, or usually, be easy to say. Still, the justification of the direction of choice will depend upon the concept of the democracy with which one began: a democracy of peoples with equal rights and privileges or a democracy of individuals. For fraternity is among persons; nationalisms—ethnic, racial, sexual, state— break it apart. Fraternity demands cosmopolitanism. In the end, it is the cosmopolitan education that makes possible conceiving all human beings as members of humanity and therefore brothers and sisters. Behind higher education, behind democracy, lies the decision whether to build on our common humanity or our uncommon roots. It is, of course, the question of the choice of moralities.

Liberty, finally, and the degree to which one prizes it, stand at issue in the choice of higher educations. That liberty is not to suit one's taste, desirable as such a liberty may be, but, through the possession of the occasions and resources necessary, to form those tastes. Only the education that provides full room for the autonomy of students and faculty in the pursuit of their positional interests can achieve that prime liberty. One might call it the liberty of selves.

Self-liberty is a risky game and hard on one. Many would demand only, as their inalienable freedom, the right to buy whatever they happen to want. The indulgent market then takes them as it finds them and, if they are lucky, provides. They are receivers—that is their virtue. Before the arrangements of things as they are, they are as little children in a seemingly endless hypermarket—to wander through the aisles unhindered is their freedom. But they are not citizens taking upon themselves their own lives. Their selves are givens. They want what they are. They are customers.

That sounds scornful; wants must be met. But when we become customers choosing among advertised brands, when we allow ourselves to be made by the media and the waves of fashion, even political liberty is subject to attenuation. For a liberty to participate in the formation of policies and in the management of the common problems of society is not, as is often enough observed, quite the same as the liberty to register what one likes and doesn't like. Political liberty requires a more active virtue than the drive to pleasure oneself so long as one harms no one else—a virtue that can arise only under the conditions of self-liberty. For the world and its possibilities change and, changing, make intrinsically problematic the ends beyond the protection of one's own skin that one will consciously and deliberately seek. Problem after problem arises that customary responses cannot handle and that require new modes of conception, new criticisms, delicate reassessments. The liberty of citizens comes down, finally, not to a right to make a loud noise and throw one's weight around—though that is inalienable—but to a participation in the making of a society one has come to realize one wants.

Those opposed to democratic liberty bring up the fickleness, the instability, the willingness to be bought off by bread and circuses, the need of the "masses" for miracle, mystery, and authority. They then derive from their realism the ultimate superiority of some preferred authoritarianism. They might better have derived, given the disasters of authoritarianisms, the centrality of a certain kind of education for a democracy—in the argument of this book, a liberal education that availed itself of the openings toward work, service, art, and politics for the sake of persons capable of the exercise of free choice.

One ought not expect too much of such an education. To indicate the choice of higher educations one would make on a democratic commitment is a long way from asserting the sufficiency of higher education to form a democracy. Even if the efforts of the higher education advocated here to develop citizens instead of information banks were supplemented, as they need to be, by the efforts of primary and secondary schools, higher education would remain a minor factor in the making of the world. Still, the question remains which way to educate, the direction to choose. There is no avoiding that question. Avoiding it, one answers.

Democratic values aside, a last, though hardly independent issue underlies the choice of a higher education: how, finally, when the chips are down, to imagine the society to which one belongs in relation to the high culture that scholars, artists, scientists, writers, and philosophers present to it. What kind of life will that society make available? What will be the range of dreams and nightmares, frustration and delight that it makes possible?

Sweetness and light are poppycock. They have less to do with the power and potency of the high culture than with high consumership. The problem of a high culture integrated into the self is the deepening of life, the troubling of it, the refinement of its consciousness. One either asks that of the higher education that ministers to that culture or one settles for a diversion separate from the business of life in society. If one settles for diversion, higher education has become useless, irrelevant. The education that offers, precisely, *polish* begs to be excommunicated, denied a place as a fundamental part of society or as a prime means for assessing the nature of its business.

To defend the integration of a high culture within a society, there is no need to play down the widespread desire in the present world economy for consumer goods or its legitimacy. There are flat out needs, universal desires, that require neither higher education nor high culture. But from that fact the choice of a straight high-tech culture and education does not follow; even defeat must be given its meaning. There are other human needs than the need to exist heavy pocketed within a bursting market.

In brief, the issue for any society is not survival and the minimal amenities, but the manner of life in surviving. It is not unusual for the arts, sciences, and the refinements of interpersonal relations to suffer under hard conditions. But whether present conditions are hard enough so that perforce they suffer, whether, indeed, even in providing for the accustomed requirements of everyday life they must do so in ways that exclude the significance of the elements of a high culture, is another matter.

That they are another matter—not a dubious cultural relativism—bars drawing the line of civilization between ourselves, the wealthy and the advanced, and those primitive others, the undeveloped, the uncivilized. We might be the barbarians. We might be the primitive, the undeveloped, the uncivilized, striving to realize that state on the highest levels of comfort. Other societies, less well situated by far, might do—have indeed done—very much better than the apologists of economic necessity and large profits might like to believe, very much better than we have done for all our unprecedented wealth and expertise.

Here is the choice, then, to which the troubles of contemporary higher education and the remedies advanced have led: whether to work for an R and D civilization with the kinds of characteristics that follow upon the minimization of liberal education and the rejection of the openings possible for higher education—whether to choose in effect a barbarism which in the sense of higher education is no civilization at all—or to expend our resources in shaping the very manner in which we pursue our subsistence and our lives. Pursuing the second course, we may come to understand what technology we really need. The achievement of that technology is not thereby precluded; science is not retarded. Rather, they are given a further dimension of meaning.

Government and private endowments want bigger and better computers and programs to figure out their trivial messages and telecommunications networks to communicate them. They aim at practicality. Stripping us for action, they insulate culture from action, reason from choice. I do not doubt that we may live that way since for the most part we have. But which way those in higher education throw what weight they have will determine their choice of educations. Which way society decides the issue will exhibit its choice of civilizations.

NOTES

Notes

CHAPTER ONE

1. My emphasis is on argument. Argument is not war; the idea is to reason together. If reasoning together is impossible, war supersedes it; to the extent that it does, the institution of higher education disappears. I assume that my indisputable cases have not disappeared.

2. See Ronald Dworkin, *Taking Rights Seriously* (Cambridge: Harvard University Press, 1978).

3. See Allan Bloom, *The Closing of the American Mind: How Higher Education Has Failed Democracy and Impoverished the Souls of Today's Students* (New York: Simon & Schuster, 1987). For an example of the justification of higher education as a source of new technologies, see Frances D. Ferguson as reported in the *New York Times*, Dec. 7, 1988, p. 16. Her position as one of four members of a panel on "Keeping America Competitive: The Role of Education" is summarized as follows: "A liberal arts education emphasizes the creative thinking needed to produce new technologies and marketing strategies, the global perspective that explains the cultural differences costing America its competitive edge, and the ethical responsibility that will help companies produce products to meet human needs." She is quoted as saying: "We have often today forsaken the focus which gave America its competitive edge, namely the emphasis on a product developed through creative thinking, innovative spirit, a global outlook, an awareness of the long-term effects of one's actions, and a developed sense of societal responsibility."

4. From Robert M. Hutchins, *The Higher Learning in America*, 1936, as quoted in *Higher Education in Transition* (3d rev. ed.), by John S. Brubacher and Willis Rudy (New York: Harper & Row, 1976), 295.

5. See Bloom, *Closing of the American Mind*, 249.

6. Ibid., 254.

7.   Ibid., 279. "Why," he asks there, "are the gentlemen more open [to philosophy] than the people?" He answers, "Because they have money and hence leisure and can appreciate the beautiful and the useless." Indeed, connoisseurs need time and money. See Martha Nussbaum's review of Bloom's book, "Undemocratic Vistas," in the *New York Review of Books*, Nov. 5, 1987.

8.   Bloom, *Closing of the American Mind*, 256.

9.   Cf. the President's Commission on Higher Education for Democracy, 1947, in *American Higher Education: A Documentary History*, ed. R. Hofstadter and W. Smith, vol. 2 (Chicago: University of Chicago Press, 1961), 979: "We shall be denying educational opportunity to many young people as long as we maintain the present orientation of higher education toward verbal skills and intellectual interests. Many young people have abilities of a different kind, and they cannot receive 'education commensurate with their native capacities' in colleges and universities that recognize only one kind of educable intelligence. . . . Traditionally the colleges have sifted out as their special clientele persons possessing verbal aptitudes and a capacity for grasping abstractions. But many other aptitudes—such as social sensitivity and versatility, artistic ability, motor skill and dexterity and mechanical aptitude and ingenuity—also should be cultivated." The extremity of the position derives more from a demand that one particular kind of institution satisfy the educational right to equal concern for everyone in the population than from the demands of the economy. But put the two together and the pressure is irresistible.

10.   Jacques Barzun, *The American University* (New York: Harper & Row, 1968), 11.

CHAPTER TWO

1.   The actual interests of the persons who happen to be students or faculty need not in fact be advanced by satisfying their interests as students or faculty. But it follows not that a census is required of those who happen to be students or faculty, only that there can be no higher education without fair rules of admission and appointment and without presenting to candidates beforehand a minimally clear idea of what they may hope to achieve at the institution.

2. See David Hume, *Enquiry Concerning the Principles of Morals*, sec. 5, pt. 2: "How, indeed, can we suppose it possible in anyone who wears a human heart that, if there be subjected to his censure one character or system of character which is beneficial, and another which is pernicious to his species or community, he will not so much as give a cool preference to the former, or ascribe to it the smallest merit or regard?" See also sec. 9, conclusion: "No selfishness, and scarce any philosophy, have force . . . sufficient to support a total coolness and indifference; and he must be more or less than a man who kindles not in the common blaze."

3. It should be clear that my argument in no way entails the "means-ends dichotomy" against which American pragmatism so long argued. That dichotomy represents a separation in principle, that ends be established independent of means because that is the nature of ends. I assume only that in the chain of means and ends breaks do in fact occur. That educational institutions can, through proper instruction, proper means, always secure their proper ends is the fiction against which we argue.

4. See Noel Annan, "Gentlemen and Players," in the *New York Review of Books*, Sept. 29, 1988, p. 63.

CHAPTER THREE

1. Sidney Hook, *Education for Modern Man: A New Perspective* (new ed.; New York: Humanities, 1973), 60. Hook also notes that "in selecting growth we are selecting a certain type or kind of development," and that "the necessity for a social frame of reference is clearly indicated" (p. 61). This, he and Dewey take to be democracy. Why? Because one assumes "an empirical approach which regards the test of consequences as decisive" (pp. 61–62). The consequences are "for weal and woe" (p. 63).

2. John Dewey, *Democracy and Education* (1916; New York: Macmillan, 1961), 53.

3. In grade school, perhaps, matters might be otherwise. Growth there might well constitute a positional interest of the children and hence of their teachers for them. That would differentiate grade school

from "higher" education where the "growth" of the individual is the individual's business, not the teacher's.

4.   Dewey, *Democracy and Education*, 54.

5.   Cf. Gerald Edelman, *Neural Darwinism* (New York: Basic Books, 1987).

6.   My formulation both here and in Point 1 takes off from George Herbert Mead's in *Mind, Self, and Society* (1934; Chicago: University of Chicago Press, 1959): "The self has a character which is different from that of the physiological organism proper. . . . It is not initially there at birth, but arises in the process of social experience and activity, that is, develops in the given individual as a result of his relations to that process as a whole and to other individuals within that process" (p. 135). The individual, we are told, "experiences himself as such, not directly, but only indirectly, from the particular standpoints of other individual members of the same social group as a whole to which he belongs. For he enters his own experience as a self or individual, not directly or immediately, not by becoming a subject to himself, but only in so far as he first becomes an object to himself just as other individuals are objects to him or in his experience; and he becomes an object to himself only by taking the attitudes of other individuals toward himself within a social environment or context of experiences and behavior in which he and they are involved" (p. 137). See also Mead, *On Social Psychology: Selected Papers*, ed. and with an Introduction by Anselm Strauss (Chicago and London: University of Chicago Press, 1964), where he tells us that the self is "an individual who affects himself as he affects another; who takes the attitude of the other insofar as he is using what we call 'intelligible speech'; who knows what he himself is saying, insofar as he is directing his indications by these significant symbols to others with the recognition that they have the same meaning for them as for him; such an individual is, of course, a phase of the development of the social form" (p. 40).

7.   The point is, of course, in a general way a Marxist one. But it is essential that this treatment not be committed either to the dialectic or to the onward progress of history. If, indeed, history moved onward and upward, "growth" would be a legitimate objective.

8.   John Dewey, *Logic: The Theory of Inquiry* (New York: Henry Holt, 1938), advanced the proposition that "inquiry is the controlled

or directed transformation of an indeterminate situation into one that is so determinate in its constituent distinctions and relations as to convert the elements of the original situation into a unified whole" (pp. 104–5). If there be inquiry into the rationality of values and decisions, as Dewey's entire enterprise aims to show, and if there be determinate criteria for a "unified whole," then the possibility of attaining it must represent a pure gamble. The gamble is on the nature of the "elements of the original situation" and the selves for which the whole is "unified." If one loses the gamble—and there is no gamble if one cannot lose—does that mean there was no inquiry?

9. For a general account of prediction problems, see James Gleick, *Chaos: Making a New Science* (New York: Viking Penguin, 1987).

10. In his systematic attack on the "dichotomy" between means and ends in all phases of human life, not only in education, Dewey made that same point the centerpiece of his philosophy. It appears in his *Experience and Nature, Logic: The Theory of Inquiry, Art as Experience,* and *Ethics.* For him the concept of growth implies it; for us the converse does not follow.

CHAPTER FOUR

1. The question raised goes beyond the nature of the interpersonal relationships to be institutionalized on campus. Computers linked to satellites, for example, might serve to include persons with whom otherwise there might be little or no communication. My argument does not block the possible uses of the devices of technology. The human larynx is a well-known communicative device. Why turn down another?

2. Plato, *The Collected Dialogues*, ed. Edith Hamilton and Huntington Cairns, trans. A. E. Taylor (Princeton, N.J.: Princeton University Press, 1973), *Laws* 2.654.

CHAPTER FIVE

1. See C. S. Peirce, "The Fixation of Belief," in *Philosophical Writings of Peirce*, ed. Justus Buchler (New York: Dover, 1955), 5–22.

2. Studies in the historical arts of China and Japan, for example, obviously might have a place. Professional preparation in astrology will not, even if another culture values astrology. Either distinctions are made or the institution disappears. The culminating educations of other cultures will, and ought to, reach very different decisions. We have no choice, however, but to use the standards of this one to determine what will be incorporated and what will not.

3. Bloom, *Closing of the American Mind*, 43, 181, 381.

4. "Liberal education," writes Bloom, "puts everything at risk and requires students who are able to risk everything" (p. 370). With this statement, the account presented here substantially agrees. There would, presumably, be less agreement on the nature of what is risked and how it is risked, and on the nature of the gains as well.

CHAPTER SIX

1. Cf. E. D. Hirsch, Jr., *Cultural Literacy: What Every American Needs to Know* (Boston: Houghton Mifflin, 1987), xiii, 2.

2. Even so, I suggest, the problem of cultural illiteracy is not a problem of the lack of information as such. Of course people don't know what they should. The remedy, however, is not therefore a spreadsheet of what they ought to know. Sufferers from anorexia would certainly be cured if only they would eat. But that end wouldn't be attained by presenting them with an adequate diet. Similarly, information is not necessarily the remedy for illiteracy.

3. See Hirsch in an exchange of letters with Herbert Kohl in the *New York Review of Books*, Apr. 13, 1989, pp. 50–51.

4. Dewey tried to establish a tight interrelationship between the idea of a justifiable education and the idea of a democratic, participatory society. He writes, "A society which makes provision for participation in its good of all its members on equal terms and which secures flexible readjustment of its institutions through interaction of different forms of associated life is in so far democratic" (*Democracy and Education*, 99). It is a society so conceived that makes the exploration of democracy appear a suitable subject for general education. At the same time, it is part of the terrain a general education would map only in the sense that it constitutes a possibility—one of many—for exploration

and criticism. Thus the relationship between that possibility and the kind of method of social decision making that utilizes the actual preferences of the members of a society in an appropriately "rational" way becomes problematic. Everything depends on the preferences; their rational summation may prove inconsistent with the ideal one hopes the summing will realize.

CHAPTER SEVEN

1. Montaigne, *The Complete Essays*, trans. Donald M. Frame (Stanford, Calif.: Stanford University Press, 1965), *Of Vanity*, 766.

2. This offers a partial explanation why, in a liberal arts curriculum, one encounters courses in poetry but not in humor. When humor is taken seriously and analyzed, the joke evaporates; the poem may be enriched.

3. Perhaps an overall Model exists for the particular Models of all languages. If there is a deep structure, we may get to it in virtue of some kind of built-in predisposition, as Noam Chomsky seems to hold, rather than through conditioning. The Models which a liberal education seeks to compose are, of course, not of the built-in type; nevertheless, they function in much the same way.

4. Dewey's discomfort with the practice of what was called "progressive education" would have been motivated, in our terms, by just the effort to substitute free expression for the acquisition and development of Models. "Doing" for him was hardly mindless or self-indulgent but the means through which the Models became part of the self. Here the means is the ballet.

5. Professional education at the university constitutes an (implicit) move toward satisfying that coherence interest by tying some of its disciplines to practices (see Chap. 9 below). There are, however, other moves that might be made as well (see Chaps. 10 and 11 below).

CHAPTER EIGHT

1. The view of the arts reflected here will be found developed in my *Reason and Controversy in the Arts* (Cleveland: Case Western Reserve University Press, 1968).

2. This is essentially the view of writers like John Dewey, George Herbert Mead, and more recently, Sidney Hook and Abraham Edel, when they attack the "dichotomy" of means and ends and look to the method of science to determine values rather than "merely" to be the means to them. In my metaphor, either the Model of science goes into the construction of the person who does the driving or means and ends are "separate."

3. Spinoza in his *Ethics* found bondage in passion and freedom in the activity of the mind that perceived necessity. The recognition of the value of the "impersonal mode" neither rejects other modes of life as necessarily bondage nor finds freedom in necessity. It is not a worldview I have been attempting to describe but a specific sort of experiencing that participation in the sciences makes available.

4. So, for example, attempts to formulate the so-called sciences of man in terms of the language and logic of the physical sciences make a considerable difference in the way those sciences are conceived; and attempts to substantiate a radical distinction between Geisteswissenschaften and Naturwissenschaften have led to very different programs for those sciences than have positivistic accounts. Of course, that very broad distinction oversimplifies the complexities of the relationships among the Models.

CHAPTER NINE

1. See John S. Brubacher and Willis Rudy, *Higher Education in Transition* (3d ed.; New York: Harper & Row, 1976), 10.

2. Ibid., 208: "No longer [after the founding of the Rensselaer Polytechnic Institute] would simple empirical techniques be sufficient to meet the intricacies propounded by the growing industrialization of the country. The application of science, not just to medicine, but to all phases of life, began to make demands on occupations which could only be met by more theoretical schooling."

CHAPTER TEN

1. William James, "The Moral Philosopher and the Moral Life," in *Essays in Pragmatism*, edited with an Introduction by Alburey Castell

(New York: Hafner Publishing Co., 1948), 80. The sentence preceding in James's text reads, "The course of history is nothing but the story of men's struggles from generation to generation to find the more and more inclusive order."

2. Of course, questions repeatedly arise whether forms of work previously taken as nonprofessional may not, as well as law and medicine, properly be assimilated into higher education and taken as professions. The boundaries between professions and nonprofessions, as is widely noticed, grow increasingly thin at crucial points; it is not germane here to locate those points.

3. See "On the Division of Labor in Production," by Friedrich Engels, in *The Marx-Engels Reader*, ed. Robert C. Tucker (New York: Norton, 1972), 321–27.

4. See Dewey, *Democracy and Education*, 308.

5. Ibid., 309.

6. Barzun, *The American University*, 237.

CHAPTER ELEVEN

1. Making arrangements for elective office on campus is not what is meant by the opening toward politics. Not, of course, that there is any objection in principle to an elected student council or class president; but, by and large, such elections have little to do with the matters of principle that turn the politicizing of the campus into a live issue.

2. For the view that indeterminacy and failure result from the nature of human societies under certain circumstances rather than simply from human ignorance and that the more one knows about a predicament the dimmer seem the chances of its resolution, see my "Abraham Edel and the Dream of Science," in *Ethics, Science and Democracy: The Philosophy of Abraham Edel*, ed. Irving Louis Horowitz and H. S. Thayer (New Brunswick, N.J., and Oxford: Transaction Books, 1987), 39–63. There is, however, no denying human ignorance and the consequent unavailability of adequate grounds for conclusions—or that wrong choices may be supported by the most impressive evidence. If only for those reasons, a rational approach to the coherence problem commits itself to the possibility of failure, a commitment which a higher education that accepts risks and uncertainty should find tolerable.

3. See Max Weber, "Politics as a Vocation," in *From Max Weber: Essays in Sociology*, trans. and ed. H. H. Gerth and C. Wright Mills (New York: Oxford University Press, 1946), 77–129.

4. Book 1 of *Laws*, in Plato, *The Collected Dialogues*, 351.

5. Dewey, *Democracy and Education*, 99.

CHAPTER TWELVE

1. Abraham Edel, *Aristotle* (New York: Dell, 1967), 131.

2. The *Meno*, in Plato, *The Collected Dialogues*, 384.

3. "We must start with the known," notes Aristotle. "But this term has two connotations: 'what is known to us' and 'what is known' pure and simple. Therefore we should start perhaps from what is known to us. For that reason to be a competent student of what is right and just, and of politics generally, one must first have received a proper upbringing in moral conduct. The acceptance of a fact as a fact is the starting point" (*Nicomachean Ethics*, trans. Martin Ostwald [New York: Library of Liberal Arts, 1962], Book 1, p. 7. Also note Book 2, p. 43: "Virtue or excellence . . . consists in observing the mean relative to us, a mean which is defined by a rational principle, such as a man of practical wisdom would use to determine it."

4. Judith N. Shklar, *Ordinary Vices* (Cambridge, Mass.: Belknap Press, 1984), 87.

5. The *Protagoras*, in Plato, *The Collected Dialogues*, 351: "What an absurd pair you are, Socrates and Protagoras. One of you, having said at the beginning that virtue is not teachable, now is bent upon contradicting himself by trying to demonstrate that everything is knowledge—justice, temperance and courage alike—which is the best way to prove that virtue is teachable. If virtue be something other than knowledge, as Protagoras tried to prove, obviously it could not be taught. But if it turns out to be as a single whole, knowledge—which is what you are urging, Socrates—then it will be most surprising if it cannot be taught. Protagoras, on the other hand, who at the beginning supposed it to be teachable, now on the contrary seems to be bent on showing that it is almost anything rather than knowledge, and this would make it least likely to be teachable."

6. Interesting works on such themes include Sisela Bok, *Lying: Moral Choice in Public and Private Life* (New York: Pantheon, 1978) and *Secrets* (New York: Pantheon, 1982), and Michael Walzer, *Just and Unjust Wars: A Moral Argument with Historical Illustrations* (New York: Basic Books, 1977).

CHAPTER THIRTEEN

1. Lee A. Daniels, "Some Top Universities in Squeeze Between Research and Academia," *New York Times*, May 10, 1989.

2. Cf. Alexis de Tocqueville, *Democracy in America* (New York: Knopf, 1945). See especially vol. 1, chaps. 1 and 3.

3. See ibid., author's preface, cx.

Index